EFFECTIVE COMMUNICATION TECHNIQUES

FOR CHILD CARE

MARY ARNOLD

COMMUNICATION

THOMSON

DELMAR LEARNING

Australia Canada Mexico Singapore Spain United Kingdom United States

THOMSON

DELMAR LEARNING

Effective Communication Techniques for Child Care
Mary Arnold

Vice President, Career Education SBU:
Dawn Gerrain

Director of Editorial:
Sherry Gomoll

Acquisitions Editor:
Erin O'Connor

Editorial Assistant:
Ivy Ip

Director of Production:
Wendy A. Troeger

Production Editor:
J.P. Henkel

Director of Marketing:
Wendy E. Mapstone

Channel Manager:
Donna J. Lewis

Cover Design:
Andrew Wright

For permission to use material from this text or product, submit a request online at http://www.thomsonrights.com

Any additional questions about permissions can be submitted by e-mail to thomsonrights@thomson.com

Library of Congress Cataloging-in-Publication Data

Arnold, Mary, 1950-
   Effective communication techniques for child care / Mary Arnold.
     p. cm.
     ISBN 1-4018-5683-7
   1. Day care centers--Administration. 2. Child care services--Administration. 3. Communication in management.
4. Business communication.   I. Title.
     HQ778.5.A76 2005
     362.71'2'0684--dc22

                                                          2004051630

NOTICE TO THE READER

Contents

Preface

When I completed my degree in education, the curriculum consisted of the basics: reading, writing, and arithmetic. Over the years I have watched the fields of education and child care branch out into exciting and dynamic new directions. Today's educators are truly child care professionals. Their skills must expand far beyond teaching our children the basics. They must be equipped to handle numerous complex social, behavioral, and professional challenges.

Over the last 25 years I have found that it is impossible to meet all of the challenges we have before us if we do not have effective communication skills. In a business where your reputation is everything, poor communication only leads to misunderstandings and unresolved conflicts. Our finely tuned education skills are not enough. If we fail to get our message across to our students, families, and staff, we simply cannot educate.

Finding information and guidance on developing communication skills is an easy task for those in business settings. However, a dearth of information exists that is directed specifically toward the child care professional. My objective in writing this book is to put together a comprehensive resource for everyone who considers themselves to be a child care professional. Whether you are obtaining an education degree, already a classroom teacher, director of a large child care center, or owner of a home-based center, you will be able to use this book to examine your present communication skills and make them more effective. Simply put, your ability to better educate others will rise to a new level.

Organization

Each chapter in this book introduces a specific and crucial aspect of communication. While the first two chapters present a basic outline for effective communication, the following chapters deal with specifics. Some may not be applicable to your situation, for example, designing a handbook if you are a classroom teacher. Still, the overall concepts can be utilized by all. It is important to remember that in an industry as dynamic as child care, you may find yourself in several different roles over your career. I suggest taking what you have experienced in each situation and using it to enhance your performance in a new role.

This book is meant to be a springboard for your thoughts and practice. While the organization resembles that of a traditional textbook, reading the text is only one of the tasks you will need to undertake. This text provides you with numerous opportunities to analyze your communication skills and apply them to real-life situations. Jot down your thoughts as you read the book and use them with your peers. Effective communication takes practice, and practice requires feedback from those around you. The ideas put forth in this text are meant to go beyond the page and into your daily routine.

Special Features

The text was designed to encourage both interaction and reflection. Throughout the text, you will find scenarios designated as "Effective Communication in Action" and "When Communication Breaks Down." These narratives are real-life situations that I have witnessed. As you read these scenarios, you should reflect on the information being presented and formulate your own opinion on how the situation could be handled. The "Effective Communication in Action" scenarios each offer one positive communication encounter, but there are numerous other effective approaches. You will begin to develop your own communication style based on your personality and experience. The "When Communication Breaks Down" narratives depict situations gone wrong.

Many of the chapters also contain various activities. The purpose of these activities is to stimulate conversation and discussion. The activities have been designed to help you evaluate your current communication style and direct you toward consistent, effective communication. As you continue to develop your communication style, you may find that your answers to these activities begin to change. This is to be expected and demonstrates that you are developing the skills needed to be an effective communicator. At the completion of the text, you may find it helpful to review your previous answers and comments to see if you would respond differently now.

You will also find role-playing exercises. You will need to put yourself in the shoes of the characters presented in each exercise. As a child care professional, you are likely to find yourself in similar situations. To gain the most from the role-playing exercise, you will want to discuss the situation with others who have also read it. One of the most important lessons of communication is that different approaches can be equally effective.

At the conclusion of each chapter you will find a Communication Progress Report. These reports present the fundamental communication goals described in the chapter. Just as you evaluate your student abilities to learn and grow over time, these Progress Reports provide an opportunity for you to evaluate your own skills. Please take a moment at the conclusion of each chapter to assess your own communication strengths and weaknesses.

Supplementary CD-ROM

Included with this text is a CD-ROM containing templates for many of the forms and documents discussed in the text. While each of these templates will need to be customized to fit your unique needs, they offer a solid foundation for your written communication efforts.

The following 34 templates have been included on the CD-ROM for your use:

1. Activity 3.1   Designing a New Teacher Orientation Checklist
2. Activity 3.2   Designing a Teacher Job Description
3. Activity 3.3   Designing a Teacher Performance Evaluation
4. Activity 3.4   Designing a Staff Feedback Evaluation
5. Activity 3.5   Designing a Family Feedback Evaluation
6. Activity 3.6   Designing a Yearly Staff Meeting Agenda
7. Activity 3.7   Designing a Monthly Staff Meeting Agenda
8. Activity 5.2   Customize the Welcome Section
9. Activity 5.3   Customize the Philosophy Section
10. Activity 5.4   Customize the Teaching Staff Section
11. Activity 5.5   Determining Your Goals and Objectives
12. Activity 5.6   Customize the Discipline Procedures Section
13. Activity 5.7   Customize the Injury Treatment Section
14. Activity 5.8   Customize the Sick Child Procedures Section
15. Activity 6.1   Creating a One-Page Policy Statement
16. Activity 6.2   Creating a Peanut Policy
17. Activity 6.3   Creating a Welcome Letter
18. Activity 6.4   Creating a Program-Specific Calendar
19. Activity 6.6   Creating a Coming Attractions Newsletter
20. Activity 6.7   Creating Effective Health Alerts: Lice
21. Activity 6.8   Creating a Friendly Payment Reminder
22. Activity 7.1   Creating a Daily Motivational Chart
23. Activity 7.2   Designing a Certificate of Accomplishment for Children
24. Activity 7.3   Designing a Certificate of Accomplishment for Adults
25. Activity 8.1   Development of the First Formal Preschool Evaluation
26. Activity 8.2   Development of the Second Formal Preschool Evaluation
27. Activity 8.4   Creating a Family Evaluation Form
28. Activity 9.2   Designing an Outline for Family Night Presentation
29. Activity 9.4   Creating a Checklist for In-Center Special Events
30. Activity 9.5   Creating a Chaperone Information Sheet
31. Activity 9.6   Preparing an Itinerary for Your Chaperones
32. Activity 9.7   Creating a Field Trip Checklist
33. Activity 9.8   Creating a Helping Hands Handout
34. Activity 10.1   Creating a Permission Form for Photograph Use

Acknowledgments

This book would not have been possible without the loving support of my family, friends, and coworkers. Thank you to my daughters, Rachel and Mandy, who both experienced being children in my child care center. Rachel was able to help me capture my life experiences and interpret them in written form. Mandy was always available with her keen insight and practical wisdom. My husband, Dave, always listened and offered solutions to my "current issue." My loving parents, Jean and Andy, who gave me the gift of a wonderful childhood. Susan Hamilton has been by my side for over ten years and has been instrumental in the development of many of my materials. Finally, I want to thank the hundreds of children who have brought smiles to my face. They are a constant reminder why being a child care professional is the most rewarding job I can imagine.

The author would like to thank the following reviewers, enlisted by Thomson Delmar Learning, for their helpful suggestions and constructive criticism:

Karin Alleman
Curriculum Coordinator
Washington, NC

Nancy Baptiste, Ed.D.
New Mexico State University
Las Cruces, NM

Patricia Capistron
Rocking Unicorn Preschool
West Chatham, MA

Vicki Folds, Ed.D.
Tutor Time Learning Systems
Boca Raton, FL

Judy Lindman
Rochester Community and Technical College
Rochester, MN

Defining the Communication Needs of Your Audiences

One of the best pieces of advice any child care center owner can be offered is this: In the child care business, you are only as good as your reputation. While it is true that all types of businesses are affected by public perception, the business of child care carries the extra burden of involving a family's greatest treasure, their child. Both good and bad news travel fast, and the source need not be a reliable one. It is possible for people who have never even met you or had any direct contact with your center to have an opinion of your business based upon second- or third-hand information about others' experiences. The way you communicate is vital to the success of your business. The need for effective communication is universal; whether you care for three children in your home or hundreds in a large center, effective communication skills are crucial to your success.

Most families do a significant amount of research before choosing a child care center. Initially, they will visit the child care center to meet with the director and teachers. However, the process does not stop there; families will also talk to neighbors, friends, and acquaintances about their thoughts on a particular center. Whether these opinions are based on factual information about the center or hearsay from other sources, the opinions of friends carry a great deal of influence when families are choosing care for their child.

Families who have had a positive experience with you will pass on the message to others. If they are unhappy with your services or felt that your center didn't meet their needs adequately, they will tell their friends and neighbors to steer clear of you. This "buzz," or word-of-mouth publicity, can mean the difference between a very successful business and a business that is simply surviving.

ACTIVITY 1.1 Identifying Your Audiences

Your first step to developing an effective communication strategy is to define your audiences. Only then can you put together a strategy for effective communication. Take a moment to identify the people with whom you frequently interact.

_____

_____

_____

_____

_____

_____

Look at your list. Is your audience larger than you initially thought? By actually writing down your various audiences, you start to gain perspective on exactly whom you are trying to reach. For most child care centers, the names you have jotted down fall into one of five categories. These categories, Current Students and Families, Staff, Future Students and Families, Neighbors, and Vendors, are all considered your audiences. Your current students and their families should be your primary audience and at the top of the list. This is the audience for which effective communication is the most crucial. These are the people who will determine the success of your business. Let's take a moment to examine each category more closely.

Audience No. 1:   Current Students and Families, Your Primary Audience

These are the people who currently patronize your business. You have an established relationship with this audience and see them regularly, if not daily. This is the audience that needs the most information about your center. Fortunately, they are also the easiest audience to reach.

The word *family* is used often throughout this book and is meant to refer to the individual or group of individuals who are invested in caring for the child. The term is not meant to be used exclusively for individuals who are related by blood, but rather means all of the people whom the child turns to for love and support. As the term *family* can be defined differently according to culture or background, you should allow the families in your center to explain to you which individuals will be involved in the care of the child.

Happy children and content families are your best advertisement. You do not want a child leaving your center with stories about a terrible day. One way to prevent this is to start each day on the right note. In the morning, have a staff member available to comfort crying children. You want to make the transition from care given by the family to care given by your center as easy as possible. Staff should be properly trained in recognizing and counseling an unhappy child. Every reasonable effort should be made to make the day a positive experience for all the children in your care. Pay careful attention to the children's reactions. If you find a majority of children respond negatively to a particular activity, consider reworking the lesson to make it a more enjoyable experience.

It is crucial to keep your families continually informed about their children and events at the center. If a child is hurt or disciplined during the day, it is the responsibility of the child care center staff to inform the family at the time of pickup. Families are entrusting you with their children, and in return they will need assurance that their children are happy, safe, and thriving. In future chapters we will discuss a variety of methods to facilitate this communication.

Families who are dissatisfied with your center will not hesitate to remove their children and place them with another center or alternate child care. They will certainly tell others of their frustration and dissatisfaction with your center, steering business away from you to your competitors.

EFFECTIVE COMMUNICATION IN ACTION

FAMILY: "My child was bitten today! What are you going to do about it?"

PLAN FOR COMMUNICATION:
1. Identify the issue.
2. Acknowledge the issue and provide a possible solution.
3. Confirm the solution is acceptable.

STAFF: "I have already discussed this situation with your child's teacher, and I want to say that I am sorry that your child had this experience. Although I know this was a scary situation for your child, biting can be a common behavior for this age group. As soon as the teacher learned about the bite, she examined the area and cleaned the skin. We placed a note in your child's mailbox to notify you of the incident. If the injury had been more serious, we would have contacted you immediately to determine if a visit to the doctor was needed. We have also spoken to the child who did the biting and talked about the right ways to express anger. Please let your child know that if he feels this might happen again, he should tell the teacher right away. I have also asked the teacher to keep a close eye on the situation. Do you have any questions for me? Is this plan acceptable to you?"

ACTIVITY 1.2 Additional Conversation

Is there any other information you feel should be included in this conversation?

_____

_____

_____

_____

_____

_____

WHEN COMMUNICATION BREAKS DOWN

FAMILY: "What time do the children leave on the field trip?"

STAFF: "I am not sure, but I will find out for you."

OUTCOME: In the hustle and bustle of the end of the day, the teacher did not get a chance to clarify the departure time with the parent. The child arrived the next day at 9:00 A.M., but unfortunately, the child's class had left for the trip at 8:30 A.M.

COMMUNICATION LESSON: Important information for upcoming events should be clearly communicated to all staff members in advance. The information should also be clearly posted on a bulletin board or in a newsletter.

Audience No. 2:   Staff

Educating your staff about your business, explaining how you want your business to function, and providing the staff with the necessary information and tools to do their job is another key to success. Employees who are informed, who feel that they are able to make a contribution, and who are trusted to interact with children and their families will help you get your message out. Try to put yourself in your employees' shoes for a minute; imagine how frustrating it would be not to be able to answer the questions posed by families. In many situations your staff will be the primary contact for the families at your center. Families should feel comfortable that your staff are able representatives of the center and reliable sources of information. It is also important to remember that an unhappy employee, just like an unhappy family, can disseminate negative messages to other staff members, families, and the community at large.

Audience No. 3:   Future Students and Families

Inevitably, children get older, so eventually you will need to replace each currently enrolled child. Therefore, you will need to develop an effective plan for attracting new families to your center. Every family that comes in contact with your center should be treated as a potential customer. Some of the most common categories of future families are:

- families of children who do not currently fit into your age range
- families who are new to your area and are seeking child care
- relatives of your current families
- other adults who accompany families into the center

EFFECTIVE COMMUNICATION IN ACTION

TELEPHONE CALLER: "I would like to enroll my child in your center."

STAFF: "I would be happy to provide you with information on our center. To whom am I speaking?"

TELEPHONE CALLER: "My name is Wanda Johnson."

STAFF: "Mrs. Johnson, our center offers a variety of programs. Can you tell me a little bit about your child so we can discuss which program will best fit your needs?"

TELEPHONE CALLER: "My son just turned one last week. I am going back to work part time and need care two days a week."

STAFF: "Mrs. Johnson, I would love to have your son in our program, but our center is licensed for children who are older than two years, nine months, and are potty trained. You need a center that offers an infant and toddler program. I know that the ABC Center offers this program."

TELEPHONE CALLER: "Thanks, I will give them a call."

STAFF: "Mrs. Johnson, we would love to have your son join our center when he gets a bit older. Are you interested in receiving more information about our center and the programs we offer?"

Initially this audience doesn't need as much detailed information as your currently enrolled families. Your goal should be simply to let them know about you and how to contact you in the future. If you have established effective communication with your current families, your solid reputation will enhance your ability to attract new families.

Audience No. 4:   Neighbors

Another important audience that is often overlooked is your neighborhood. Take a glance back at your list of people with whom you routinely interact. Did you remember to include the neighbors of your business? The location of your center has a direct impact on the type of neighbors you need to consider.

- Is your child care center home based? A center located in a residential area has its own set of considerations. Your neighbors may have issues with parking, blocked driveways, and noise from outdoor play areas. You may also face regulation from city zoning ordinances or deed restrictions.

WHEN COMMUNICATION BREAKS DOWN

FAMILY: "The parking is so bad. I am late because there is nowhere to park."

STAFF: "It is because of the drive-through at the business next door. I will go and take care of it right now."

OUTCOME: The center director politely walked next door to the first driver waiting in line and asked if he could move closer to the curb so the patrons of the center could park their cars. The owner of the drive-through witnessed this interaction and came outside to tell the director to leave his customers alone. Several center families witnessed this heated interaction.

COMMUNICATION LESSON: This type of logistical problem should have been anticipated and dealt with proactively rather than reactively. A plan with the adjoining business can be discussed and implemented prior to the situation affecting the customers of either business.

- Is your child care center located in a commercial location or a stand-alone facility surrounded by other businesses? You need to consider if your families are going to find nearby businesses friendly or threatening to the children. Businesses such as a drug rehabilitation center, a liquor store, a bar, or a homeless shelter may cause concern for prospective families. However, many types of neighboring businesses could be an asset to your busy families by offering one-stop convenience. Businesses that could potentially help working families might include a dry cleaner, a take-out restaurant, a video rental store, or a gift shop.

In either setting, pickup and drop-off times can offer unique challenges. You need to consider if families picking up children at peak times will restrict traffic flow or block access to neighboring businesses. Working out a traffic and parking plan with your neighbors and communicating the plan to your families can mean the difference between a great or an adversarial relationship with those businesses closest to you. Ignoring a difficult situation will not make it go away.

Your child care center is in competition with other facilities and schools. Competition, however, doesn't necessarily mean you must have an adversarial relationship. Working together with other child care centers in your immediate area can benefit everyone. One benefit of a mutual working relationship with other centers is the flexibility to refer children to one another. This situation could arise with a sibling of a current family who is too young for your program or a child who has special needs and therefore is better suited to a different environment. This type of collaborative relationship would work well between a child care center that accepts only potty-trained children age three or older and a home-based center focused exclusively on infants and toddlers. Families who inquire at the child care center about infant care are referred to home-based child care facilities. When many of the referred children reach age three, they will leave the home-based setting for the larger center, where they will be provided with a more structured learning environment. It is always a good business practice to have a place where you can refer school-age children. Establish a good relationship with local public schools. In most cases, you will refer school-age children to the neighborhood public school. Having reciprocal support from area schools can be very beneficial. However, for the families who are looking for alternatives to the public schools, you should also have information available on placement in private elementary schools.

Audience No. 5:   Vendors

Venders are sometimes an overlooked audience. Everyone from your cleaning service to outside programs brought into your center for the children (art, music, dance, etc.) has an opinion about you and will share it with others. There are several issues to consider when thinking about your relationship with vendors. Do you pay vendors promptly? If they are working on-site, is their area neat and clean? Are they treated like an important component to the success of your business? Do families ask for this service? Do the vendors follow your basic philosophy on child care? Do they have a discipline policy?

In addition, the vendors that you choose to serve your center will send messages to another primary audience, the families. If you decide to bring in extracurricular programs, be sure to do some research to ensure that reputable organizations run these programs. Although the programs may not be completely under your control, they do represent you and your center. The last thing you want is dissatisfied families unhappy about some program you have added. Consider the instructors: do they dress and behave in a professional manner? Are the children excited about attending the programs? Are you charging children extra tuition to attend these programs? Are the vendors privately insured or are their services covered under an umbrella policy for your program? Reactions from your students and families will give you a good idea about how beneficial these extracurricular activities are to your bottom line. A poorly run and mismanaged extracurricular program will be a turnoff to your students and families. This could also be a drain on your finances.

In the broadest sense, everyone in your community will have an opinion about you, whether they actually have had experience with you or not. Your relationship with all of the five audiences and how effectively you communicate with each will determine how the community as a whole views you and your business.

Now that we have examined each of the audiences, Current Students and Families, Staff, Future Students and Families, Neighbors, and Vendors, let's take the next step in the process of effective communication. Next you have to determine what you want your audiences to know about you. You must determine your message, or the overall impression you wish to present to the community.

ACTIVITY 1.3 Define Who You Are

Answering the following questions will help you to define the focus of your business.

How do you visualize your business?_____

_____

_____

Do you consider yourself an affordable child care center? If your rates are higher

than those of competitors, what advantages do you offer to offset this?_____

_____

_____

Are you an academically oriented center?_____

_____

_____

What policies, programs, equipment, and curriculum do you use to identify your

program?_____

_____

_____

What are the strengths of your center?_____

_____

_____

In which areas can your center be improved?_____

_____

_____

This isn't about making promises you can't deliver, but rather about examining your entire operation to determine its strengths and weaknesses. The message you want to present must accurately reflect how you conduct your business.

The next step is to focus on the strengths that you feel best serve your primary audience and determine how to best communicate these strengths. You may also want to work on some of your weak areas. Find ways to improve your center, but just as important, be sure to let your audiences know about the improvements you're making. These improvements could involve enhancing your curriculum, offering teacher training, or upgrading your physical facility.

You've taken a good, objective look at your business. Now you need to get some additional input from your staff, currently enrolled families, and friends.

ACTIVITY 1.4 How Do Others See You?

Ask members of your four target audiences the questions you just answered about your own center and compare their responses to yours. Do any audiences answer the questions significantly differently than you did? If so, you have just identified one area you need to work on to strengthen communication within your center.

So now you have determined what you do well and identified some areas you would like to improve. You've discovered your core message. Now how do you get this message to your multiple audiences?

Every audience has differing needs in terms of information about your program. The families of currently enrolled children are your primary audience. They need to know the most about your business. This would include your center policies and procedures, fees, acceptable behavior expectations, drop-off and arrival times, and everything else families need to know about the type of care their child will receive. Your staff needs to know, and be able to communicate, this same information to the families as well. The messages your families get from you and your staff must be consistent.

The messages you give to the children in your care are based on the information given to the families. Children need to know the daily routine. They need to know what is expected of them and the consequences of not following the rules. Children need loving consistency in their environment, so teachers and staff members will spend a good part of their day helping the children learn the center's routine. In the case of families of current students, you bring your potential audience to you. This audience asks for, and is receptive to, many forms of communication from you. After all, they entrust their child to your center for a good portion of the day.

Other audiences are more challenging to reach, but don't require nearly as much information. Families of potential students can be reached through paid advertising, special events such as open houses, flyers, newspaper articles, and other vehicles that provide enough information that families can contact you if they are interested in your services.

Your business neighbors are easy to find. A great way to establish a positive relationship with neighboring businesses or residences is a personal visit. Introduce yourself and explain a little about your business. After the initial meeting, you can call to set up additional meetings to discuss issues that arise such as parking or traffic. It helps tremendously if you are proactive and address any potential issues early, before small irritations grow to gigantic problems.

By identifying your audience and your message, you have taken the first steps toward effective communication. Now you need to take care to avoid the most common pitfalls in effective communication. By understanding the challenges, you are better equipped to avoid falling into these communication traps.

Ten Common Pitfalls in Effective Communication for Child Care Centers

- offering an ill-defined message or image for your business
- making promises or claims that are untrue or undeliverable
- wasting time and money getting detailed messages to people outside your primary audience
- not giving your primary audience enough information
- providing inconsistent messages
- poorly informing staff
- choosing the wrong vehicle to get your messages out
- being reactive rather than proactive
- assuming your audience already knows the information
- providing poorly produced materials

Offering an ill-defined message or image for your business. If you haven't taken time to examine your business philosophy and determine your strengths and weaknesses, you won't be able to tell your clients and prospective clients exactly what you can offer. In fact, you need to know precisely who you are so you can sell yourself to others. You have to be able to distinguish yourself from the competition. You must be able to stand out.

Making promises or claims that are untrue or undeliverable. Hand-in-hand with undefined messages are messages that are simply not true. There's no quicker way to drive customers away than to make claims and promises that you cannot, or do not expect to, deliver. If your promotional literature says that you provide gourmet meals to the children in your care but the reality is that lunch is usually boxed macaroni or hot dogs, families will not be happy. Your message about the gourmet lunches was not true. If you had no intention of providing gourmet lunches, either don't mention lunch or be honest with your customers and publish accurate menus.

Wasting time and money getting detailed messages to people outside your primary audience. You've spent a great deal of time preparing advertisements and other promotional materials and are anxious for everybody to see it, so you hand it out at a local mall show. However, patrons at a casual mall show or community festival don't

WHEN COMMUNICATION BREAKS DOWN

A worst-case scenario involves a home-based child care center. The center ran into difficulties over a driveway shared with neighboring homeowners. The center had been licensed and operational for several years. The neighbors had no problems with the child care center or daily traffic on the shared driveway until a few years later, when they decided to sell their property. The homeowners felt that the shared driveway, traffic, and parking issues associated with the neighboring child care center would have a negative impact on the selling price of their home.

The homeowners took the case to court, petitioning the court to shut down the child care center entirely. Thus, a friendly neighborhood setting became a battleground. The court did not shut down the child care center as the homeowners had hoped, but reduced the maximum number of children that could be served at the center. The homeowners sold their property and moved away. The child care center owners spent a large sum of money in legal fees, construction for the new driveway, and costs of opening an additional center.

COMMUNICATION LESSON: Do your research, including legal issues, prior to solidifying your business plan. Hire an expert to help on any complicated issues. Make it a priority to know your neighbors and work proactively with this audience to establish a relationship of mutual respect. When the lines of communication are established early, all parties involved have a better chance of addressing issues before they get to the stage of irreparable disrepair.

need the type of detailed information that would be found in a handbook. Most of the promotional literature you hand out at a show will end up in the trash. A business card, a brief brochure, or perhaps a current center newsletter would all be just as effective as an expensive handbook. If people are truly interested, schedule an appointment for a visit to the center. The appropriate time to give a copy of your handbook is when families actually come into your center for a visit. You can use the handbook to spark discussion with families or to go over any issues of concern. Use your resources wisely and, while giving accurate information, balance your audiences' "need to know" with the cost of reaching them.

Not giving your primary audience enough information. If your families don't know about your vacation policy, they aren't going to be able to meet your requirements. Likewise, if they are unsure of your hours of operation or any other facet of your business, it will cause frustration for all concerned. Make sure your families are informed about every detail of your center that applies to their child and their requirements for attending your child care facility.

The families of your students are busy, just like you are. They don't like to find out that their child needs a festive holiday hat the day before a performance. In many instances, you may have given the child all of the necessary information but it was lost somewhere between the center and the car or home. You need to send the same message in several different forms. If a message is important, post it on the door, put it in a newsletter, and make a bulletin board display. You need to anticipate the confusion.

Providing inconsistent messages. A successful communication plan calls for uniform messages to all your different audiences. You cannot tell one set of families it's OK if their child isn't "quite" potty trained and then deny another child admission to your center because he is at the same stage. This will come back to haunt you. Having defined procedures in writing helps you present a consistent message so all your clients feel they're being treated fairly.

Poorly informing staff. Your employees are the heart of your child care center. They are the core of your business. They care for the children and interact with families on a daily basis. If your staff is ill-informed or unfamiliar with your policies and procedures, clients will soon question your capability to care for their child. A poorly trained staff will make a poor impression and will give families incorrect or inconsistent information.

If staff members are unable to answer questions about the center or center programs and families are forced to seek you out on even minor questions, the families may wonder just how capable and qualified the people watching their children are.

Choosing the wrong vehicle to get your messages out. A four-color brochure and 10 radio spots might make you feel like you've finally "arrived" in the world of advertising. However, you need to consider if this is the most effective way to reach potential families. Do the people who will place their children in your care listen to the radio station where you placed the ads? Do they listen at the times the ads are running? How will you distribute the brochures? A well written, professionally designed brochure in four colors can be an excellent marketing tool, but not if it sits in the bottom drawer. Would the money spent on brochures be more effective if you'd produced a center handbook or a monthly newsletter?

Being reactive rather than proactive. You want to be a proactive communicator. If you feel that traffic patterns in front of your child care center will be a problem at 3:00 P.M., you can be proactive by discussing this issue with neighbors before one of them brings it to your attention. If you have a child with behavior issues, you can be a proactive communicator by contacting the families for a parent-teacher conference to discuss possible underlying causes of the behavior and come up with possible solutions.

Assuming your audience already knows the information. You've been using the same policy manual for the past five years and know every word. Your staff has been with you for a long time, and they are well versed in your center's policies. But you can't assume that your families know the policies. More often than not, families will read or skim over the policy manual, yet once the first snow day arrives, they will have many questions. Small reminders, a brief newsletter, or phone calls if needed can all reinforce the information to new families and will help them learn and understand your policies.

Providing poorly produced materials. Whether you type your center newsletter yourself or pay a writer and graphic artist for professional production, make sure that your materials are well written and error free. There's nothing worse than a piece of writing that's full of grammatical, spelling, and punctuation errors. Take the extra time to proofread all your materials before they're printed.

If you are in the business of caring for children, you are very dependent upon your image. You may have a wonderful child care program, trained, caring staff, and a fabulous facility, but if public perception is that you don't provide good care, clients will stay away. You have to let people know who you are and how your business can help them. You are in control of your image and the messages that you send to the community. This can only occur after you have taken the needed time to analyze your audience and determined what you would like your audience to know about you.

Communication Progress Report

Skill or Task	Range of Abilities		
	ALMOST ALWAYS	EMERGING SKILL	WILL LEARN
I can identity my five audiences.	☐	☐	☐
A well developed plan for tailoring communications based on the audience is in place.	☐	☐	☐
Multiple avenues of communication have been established for current students and families.	☐	☐	☐
The majority of current students and families are pleased with services provided.	☐	☐	☐
The staff is well educated about all center policies.	☐	☐	☐
A majority of the staff are proud of the center and pleased to be a part of it.	☐	☐	☐
Multiple strategies for reaching new students and families are in place.	☐	☐	☐
The center has strong, positive relationships with the community.	☐	☐	☐
Vendors are good representatives of the center.	☐	☐	☐
The focus of the business is well defined.	☐	☐	☐
Strengths and weaknesses of the center have been identified.	☐	☐	☐

2

The Six C's of Communication

COMING ATTRACTIONS

- How to identify and use the three most important elements of good communication

- How to identify and avoid the three mistakes that can sabotage good communication

- How to use real-life scenarios to examine situations from multiple perspectives

In the business world, how you say something is as important as what you say. Each time you interact with a family, staff member, vendor, or child you are building upon your reputation. While the topic will change with each conversation, there are three common elements you can use to ensure the message you are projecting to others is one of professionalism. Your message should always be *clear*, *consistent*, and *caring*. Equally important as the three positive elements of communication are the three most commonly made mistakes. Although your message may have been well intentioned, by including elements of *confrontation*, *conflict*, or *carelessness*, you will no doubt overshadow your message and leave your audience confused and possibly angry. The first step in improving your communication skills is to learn about techniques that you can use in real-life situations. You will then have to put these ideas into action and determine the approaches that will work best in your environment. First let's discuss the three positive elements of communication, which you should attempt to use in each of your communications.

Positive Communication Element No. 1: Clarity

Have you ever fumbled in an explanation to another person, even when the situation you wanted to describe was clear in your mind? Of course this has happened to you—it has happened to everyone at one point or another. The leap from mind to mouth can be a complex one, but it is an important skill for effective communication. In order to be effective, your audience must understand your message. Before an important conversation, take a few minutes to prepare; you can jot down notes and examples if you need. As child care providers, we are often responsible for initiating difficult conversations with families. If you plan on approaching a family about their child's behavioral problems, you need to be prepared with specific examples. Use terms that are easily understood by all, not just by child care professionals, and encourage your audience (in this case, the family) to speak up and ask questions.

Although the following discussion may be commonplace between child care professionals, the technical language does not provide a clear message to the family. The family may leave the conference unsure about the terms *developmental appropriateness* and phonetics and wondering what in the world is an SLP? The same conversation can be simplified to improve its clarity; it is also important to ask the family if they have any questions. Some families may not feel comfortable asking questions on their own for fear they may be seen by the teacher as uneducated about their child and appropriate behaviors. As a result, the teacher's message, which is to work on reading skills at home and seek evaluation for the lisp, may go unnoticed. The same conversation can be reworded so the message is clear.

In the second example, the teacher uses language that is easier for her audience to understand. She also provides examples and allows the family an opportunity to ask questions or request further information. The child is much more likely to benefit from the second conversation.

Positive Communication Element No. 2: Consistency

In the child care business, you have to expect that your audiences will talk to each other, and in some cases make comparisons about the messages they have received from you. This is why it is so important to have consistency among your communications on any

WHEN COMMUNICATION BREAKS DOWN

A kindergarten teacher has called a conference with the family of one of her students. Samantha, the student, has been experiencing increasing difficulties in keeping up with the curricula; in addition, she has a pronounced lisp and may require special services to address the language problem. The teacher presents the situation to the family in the following manner:

"I have concerns that Samantha is struggling with the kindergarten curricula. The curricula have been designed to be developmentally appropriate for five-year-olds, with an emphasis on phonetics rather than whole reading. I think that Samantha may benefit from doing some additional work at home with you on these skills. In addition, I have concerns about her language and would recommend a consultation with an SLP for further evaluation."

EFFECTIVE COMMUNICATION IN ACTION

"I wanted to speak with you about some issues I have been noticing with Samantha. She has been having a very difficult time keeping up with the rest of the class, especially when it comes to reading. For example, yesterday I gave the children a copy of this story to read. [Teacher hands the family a copy of the story.] It is expected that most kindergartners would be able to read this story on their own. Samantha had a very difficult time finishing the story. I think that it would be helpful if she had some one-on-one time with you at home working on phonetics. Phonetics is a process in which children learn to read by sounding words out. Let me show you how I would help Samantha learn to read this story using phonetics. [Teacher demonstrates.] Do you have any questions about this? Would you like me to do another demonstration?

In addition, I think that it is important to discuss Samantha's speech. I am sure you have noticed that she has some problems making *th* and *st* sounds. This is common in children, but she should visit a professional who can evaluate her speech and work with her on any problem areas. These specialists are called Speech and Language Pathologists. Here is the name of one in our area who has worked with some other children in the program."

OUTCOME: The teacher explained how children learn to read, using an understandable method. She offered the family suggestions and solutions, which made them feel more comfortable about their child's reading problems.

given topic. It is surprising how small incidents can trigger bad feelings if favoritism is suspected. Take a good look at all sides of any situation before you decide to "bend the rules" a bit. If you make an exception for one family or staff member, you may be overwhelmed with requests for similar exceptions.

Consistency is especially important when you have published your policies and procedures in a handbook or other written document. We will be discussing handbooks in detail in Chapter 5, but for now it is important to keep in mind that before you commit anything to paper, you must be sure that you are committed to following and enforcing the policies.

ACTIVITY 2.1 Creating Consistent Messages

Consider the following real-world scenarios. Take a minute to write down your ideas about how the issues can be handled in a way that is both consistent and considerate of the needs of your audience.

SCENARIO: Suppose a family has approached you about bringing in a special birthday snack for their four-year-old. They plan to prepare chocolate chip and peanut butter cookies. Your handbook explicitly states that no nut products may be brought into the school because many children are allergic to nuts. The family has checked with the teacher and confirmed that none of the children in the class has a nut allergy. Therefore, they believe an exception can be made in the case of this special occasion.

HOW WOULD YOU HANDLE THIS SCENARIO?

_____

_____

_____

POSSIBLE RESPONSE TO THE SCENARIO: Many families may not understand the rationale behind some of the child care center's policies. It may be useful to explain that some children may have a severe allergic reaction by simply coming in contact with another child who has nut oil on her hands. The policy is not meant to be overly restrictive but it is a necessary measure to keep all children at the center safe. Perhaps the family can make a birthday activity out of making and serving the favorite chocolate chip and peanut butter cookies at home. However, for the well-being of all of the children in the center, the family cannot be permitted to bring in any items containing nuts.

SCENARIO: A teacher has made a request to be scheduled for the 7:00 A.M. to 3:30 P.M. shift every Friday during the summer months. This is the favorite shift for all staff members, especially during the summer. Typically the schedule is planned on a rotating basis, allowing each teacher one early Friday shift per month. The teacher who has made this request has a father who is recovering from a stroke and needs constant care.

The family is having a difficult time finding someone who can help out on Friday afternoons. The teacher believes that given these extenuating circumstances, an exception should be made to allow her to keep the preferred Friday shift.

HOW WOULD YOU HANDLE THIS SCENARIO?

_____

_____

_____

_____

POSSIBLE RESPONSE TO THE SCENARIO: There are many different angles from which this situation can be viewed. If you were to be governed by consistency alone, you would likely respond that unfortunately the teacher will have to work the shifts as scheduled. She will be permitted one early Friday per month, the same allotment as all other staff members. However, given the circumstances, you may be tempted to allow the teacher the time she needs to be with her sick father. Before making this decision, however, it is important to be mindful of how greatly this will impact your other staff members. Others may also have important reasons to keep the schedule as is. You could suggest that the teacher speak to the other staff members on an individual basis about their willingness to give up their early Friday shift. No one should be forced to relinquish the early shift, but if one teacher is willing to do so, this could be arranged. If this is the approach you take, you need to be aware that other staff members will remember the flexibility in scheduling and may request a similar scenario for themselves at some point in the future. If you allow the exception to be made in this one situation, you need to be prepared to treat future instances in a consistent manner.

Positive Communication Element No. 3:   Caring

The fundamental drive behind all great child care centers is a genuine love for children. Children learn best in an environment of support and respect. In the same way, communication occurs best in an environment where the audience feels that their needs are important and cared about. In order to be an effective communicator, you first must master the skill of listening to others. Take the time to fully understand what the other person is trying to tell you. Ask for further explanation if the message is not clear to you.

One way to physically demonstrate to your audience that you care about what they are saying is through body language. You should look directly at the person who is speaking to you. Demonstrate that the person has your entire focus by stopping whatever activities you were performing. If you look at your watch or continue to type, you will give the impression that you have other tasks that are more important. You need to give others the same respect for their time that you demand for yours. Be mindful of

WHEN COMMUNICATION BREAKS DOWN

A family wants to speak with the teacher about a problem their child has been having with another child in the class. Unfortunately, the family arrived at a time when the teacher was attending to a crying child. Although the teacher was listening to the family's concerns, she was not able to take her eyes off the crying child. The family stood over the teacher, who remained seated on the floor. The family left feeling as though the teacher might have too many other responsibilities and that their child might be better suited to another classroom. The teacher felt as though this was a productive conversation, which served to make her more aware of the interactions between the two children in the future and more ready to intervene when necessary.

how you position your body in relation to the person with whom you are speaking. If your audience is sitting down, consider coming down to that level as a symbolic gesture showing that you are both equals in this discussion. When greeting a new arrival, you should always rise, offering a firm handshake and a welcoming "hello." Try to make others feel at ease around you by maintaining a pleasant and calm demeanor, even during difficult discussions. It is a good idea to have an area in the center where you can go for private discussions. As child care providers, we are often privy to personal information about our families. You can better facilitate important discussions if you have a quiet, private area where everyone can take a moment to relax and focus on the issue at hand. Always ask for the families' opinions and recollections of what was successful in the past.

In today's business world, you need to be careful that your actions do not make others feel uncomfortable. Many people in a professional setting are not comfortable with any sort of direct physical contact, with the exception of a handshake. You should never touch the arm or leg of another person while interacting, even though this is a frequent occurrence between friends. Be sure to allow your audience the personal space they need to feel at ease.

This simple scenario illustrates how quickly misunderstandings can arise. It is possible that the family in this situation would approach the director to request a classroom change for their child. It is likely that the teacher would be surprised and unsure of the reasoning behind this request.

You have now had an opportunity to review the three elements of communication that should be incorporated in each interaction with your audience. When you have communications that are *clear*, *consistent*, and *caring*, you are helping to ensure that your message is effectively relayed to others. We will now review the three negative communication techniques—*confrontation*, *conflict*, and *carelessness*. You should work to banish these 3 C's from your communication, as they lead to confusion and bad feelings.

EFFECTIVE COMMUNICATION IN ACTION

The teacher is approached by a family wishing to speak about their child. Unfortunately, the teacher is attending to the needs of a crying child and unable to fully focus on the family and the conversation. The teacher explains that she wants to be able to take the time to fully discuss the family's concerns but is unable to do so at this moment. She asks the family if they are willing to wait for ten minutes while she calms the crying child and finds another teacher to supervise the class. If the family is unable to wait, the teacher requests that they set up another time to sit down and work out the issues. She lets the family know that she understands this is an important conversation and wants to be able to give them her full attention. The teacher and the family meet at a later time in a quiet area, where they can sit comfortably and discuss the issues that have been concerning the family. During the conversation, the teacher is careful that her focus remain on the family at all times. She makes eye contact with the family and asks relevant questions. The teacher and the family work together to find a plan that is suitable for all involved.

OUTCOME: These few extra steps let the family recognize that the teacher cares about their concerns. The teacher will be able to respond appropriately to the needs of the child.

Negative Communication Element No. 1:   Confrontation

Your word choices can make or break your conversation. You should choose words and phrases that are nonjudgmental. Try to avoid words with strictly negative connotations; such as *bad, wrong,* or *I want.* The focus of every communication should be what is best for the child, the family, the teacher, or the center as a whole. You want to create an environment that facilitates discussion, not confrontation. When people feel they are being confronted, they often become defensive and unwilling to listen to what others have to say.

Confrontations often occur when emotions override reason. If you are feeling overwhelmed by your emotions, it is your duty as a professional to take a step back to reevaluate the issues at hand. It is perfectly acceptable to ask for a moment to collect your thoughts or even to arrange another time to continue the discussion. It is impossible to take statements back, so make sure that you never allow yourself to become so overcome by emotion that you make remarks you will regret later.

Almost all families possess a "mother bear" instinct: They feel a need to protect their child at all costs. This instinct can lead to confrontation, but as a child care professional, you should be equipped to handle such situations. If you are confronted by an angry family member, you should let him or her know that you understand that it is important to sit down and discuss the issues at hand. Ask the family if you can schedule a time to meet when you can give them your undivided attention. This slight postponement will give you some time to collect your thoughts and will also allow the family some "cooling-down time." During the discussion, you should keep in mind that you are a professional and should never raise your voice or use inflammatory language, even if the family is not abiding by the same rules. It may be necessary to have another individual present to witness the conversation in the event accusations are made at a later date. If you ever feel threatened, it is your right to quickly end the conversation and remove yourself from the situation. Moreover, if you ever feel as though an individual has become a threat to you and the children in your care, it is your right to ask him or her to leave the center immediately. If this request is not followed, call the police for assistance. Although these are unlikely scenarios, it is important to be prepared. When children are involved, emotions are easily provoked, but it is the responsibility of the child care provider to remain calm and in control of the situation.

ACTIVITY 2.2 Handling Confrontation

Consider the following real-world scenarios. Take a minute to write down your ideas about how the issues could be handled so as to minimize confrontation and find an acceptable solution for all involved.

SCENARIO: As a teacher you have worked diligently on your lesson plans for an upcoming unit. You showed your plans to another teacher in order to receive feedback. Today you walk into your coworker's classroom to find your unit posted on this teacher's bulletin board. You are furious that she has taken your plans and claimed them as her own.

HOW WOULD YOU HANDLE THIS SCENARIO?

_____

_____

_____

_____

POSSIBLE RESPONSE TO THE SCENARIO: Take a minute to collect yourself and resist the urge to confront your coworker with, "How dare you steal my ideas!" Doing so will only result in an emotional response and will not help bring resolution to the situation. If the children are beginning to arrive, you will need to wait to have the conversation until you have a quiet minute to yourselves. When you do approach this coworker, do it in a manner that acknowledges that you know she has used your ideas and others may also know that the original ideas were yours but does not put her on the defensive. For example, you could say: "I see that you used my ideas for your bulletin board. I am glad you thought they were good ones. I had also shown them to some other teachers and they agreed the children would enjoy the project. Maybe in the future we could work together to plan a lesson and put together the bulletin board. Do you have any ideas for next month's unit?"

SCENARIO: A father of one of your four-year-old students storms up to you at drop-off time. Yesterday his child reported that she was pinched by another child in the classroom. The father shows you a large bruise on his daughter's forearm. You were not aware of the incident; the child never cried or reported the pinching to you. The father is furious that you were not paying close enough attention to his daughter. He questions your credentials as a teacher and your ability to maintain a safe environment for his child. He informs you that he plans to make a formal complaint to the director of the center regarding your "negligence."

HOW WOULD YOU HANDLE THIS SCENARIO?

_____

_____

_____

_____

POSSIBLE RESPONSE TO THE SCENARIO: You should let the father know that he has every right to report the situation to the director. If he feels it would be useful, you can arrange a meeting between the family, yourself, and the director. At this point you need to let the father know that you are sorry this happened to his daughter. In addition to apologizing, you can reassure him that you do keep a careful eye on all of the children. If you had seen the incident or had his daughter reported it to you, you would have followed the appropriate procedures of first aid. The family should be aware that it is the policy of the center to promptly report all incidents to the families. Ask if you can sit down together with his daughter to discuss what she can do if this ever happens again. Let the child know, in the presence of her father, that she should always tell the teacher right away if she is hurt by another child.

Negative Communication Element No. 2:   Conflict

It is inevitable that there are going to be situations in which conflict arises. You should strive to work with the other party involved to work through the conflict. Ensure that your position is clear, consistent, and caring and that you are not confronting the other party. All parties should be adequately informed about all aspects of the issue and

WHEN COMMUNICATION BREAKS DOWN

At the final conference for the four-year-old program, you meet with a family to discuss the progress their child has made over the past year in your class-room. You inform the family that their son is not ready to graduate to the kindergarten program and should remain in the fours class for another year. The family is shocked at this news and unwilling to discuss the prospect of their child not starting kindergarten in the fall. They are angered that this has not been brought to their attention earlier, although you remind them that throughout the year, you did make some passing references to their son's maturity level. The family informs you that their son will be attending kindergarten next year and they see your recommendation to repeat the fours program as a sign of your failure as a teacher.

EFFECTIVE COMMUNICATION IN ACTION

The teacher sits down with the family of one of her four-year-old students. She knew this was going to be a difficult conversation, so she prepared well for it. The teacher informs the family that she believes it is in the best interest of their child to repeat the Fours program. She offers many examples as to why the child is not emotionally ready to move on to kindergarten. This is a discussion that she has had with the family on multiple occasions throughout the year. The teacher impresses on the family how much more their child will get out of the kindergarten program if he has another year to develop within the preschool curricula. The teacher ensures that the family knows that this recommendation has nothing to do with their child's future intellectual or emotional abilities. It is simply a matter of maturity and readiness, and it is not uncommon for children to start kindergarten at age six instead of age five. Although the family is not surprised by this news, they remain displeased. They are able to ask questions and have agreed to think about the teacher's recommendation over the course of the summer. The teacher lets the family know she understands that the ultimate decision is up to them. She asks them to feel free to contact her if they wish to have any further discussions.

should have a chance to ask questions and even take some time away to think about the possible solutions. Even when you are using good communication skills, it is possible that battle lines will be drawn. It may be that you and a family or you and another staff member just don't see eye-to-eye on a situation. Even if this occurs, however, you need to maintain your professional attitude.

The very first step in resolving conflict is to identify the issues that everyone agrees upon. In many cases, everyone will agree that the best interest of the child is of paramount importance. However, conflict can arise by differing ideas on how to best meet that goal. Fortunately, the conflicting sides may have more in common than first meets the eye. Take a moment at the onset to outline your agreements so you can focus your energies on areas where differences exist.

If the conflict is between a family regarding their child, you must respect the fact that the ultimate decision-making power lies with the family. As a child care professional, you may offer advice and state your opinion, giving examples to back up your position, but if a family chooses not to follow your advice, you must respect their decision. If the conflict occurs between two staff members, it may be that they just need to respect each other's differing opinions and agree to disagree. If the issue is so critical that a decision must be made, a supervisor should be brought into the conversation. If the final outcome does not support your side, you need to accept the decision without resentment and be willing to overcome your differences.

In this situation, the teacher has confronted the family with important news that ultimately leads to conflict. The teacher's message also lacks consistency; the family should have been informed repeatedly throughout the course of the year that their child might not be ready for kindergarten in the fall. The emotional response of the family does not allow for any discussion, nor does it give the teacher an opportunity to clarify her position.

The ability to handle conflict and resolve it appropriately is a difficult skill to teach. Familiarization with the handbook and the center policies is only part of the preparation needed to handle and resolve conflict. Your staff members also need to be able to think on their feet. Staff members need to be prepared for questions that cannot be answered by pointing to a policy outlined in the handbook. You will also need to be prepared to deal with conflict that arises through no fault of your own.

ACTIVITY 2.3 Conflict Resolution

Consider the following real-world scenario. Take a minute to write down your ideas about how the issue could be handled in a professional, calm manner.

SCENARIO: You are a classroom teacher involved in storytime when a parent interrupts with: "You lost my child's lunch box! I need you to find it right now so we can leave!"

HOW WOULD YOU HANDLE THIS SITUATION?

_____

_____

_____

_____

POSSIBLE RESPONSE TO SCENARIO: As a child care professional you need to continue to present yourself as calm, caring, informed, and in control, despite this conflict. Whenever a conflict arises, you need to ensure that you are correctly interpreting the real issue at hand. One of the easiest ways to accomplish this is to repeat the problem presented to you. In situations such as this, you may feel that this step is unneeded, but it will serve you well in more complex scenarios. Here you could restate the problem like this, "I am sorry, did you say that you need help in finding the missing lunch box?" Once you have confirmed the conflict at hand, you can begin the steps needed to resolve it. Your first step in resolving this conflict is to provide the family with information that may help them. Let the family know all of the possible places they should look for the missing lunch box: Could it have been placed in the wrong cubby, left at the lunch table, be hidden under the coats? You will then need to acknowledge their emotions. Let them know that you understand their frustration, especially when this happens at the end-of-the-day rush. Finally, you will need to offer the family a solution. In this situation, you could offer to check for the lunch box ahead of time, when you put away the nap supplies. In the future, if the lunch box is missing, you will have time to look for it before the end-of-the-day rush.

ACTIVITY 2.4 Charting Your Conflict Resolution Skills

One way to improve your conflict resolution skills is to reflect on and evaluate how you have handled past situations. Sometimes we make statements in the heat of the moment that we would avoid otherwise. Reflection on these situations can help us learn to make better choices the next time we have a similar conflict. You can also use this exercise to initiate an open discussion about conflict resolution. Ask staff members to share a situation where they feel they successfully resolved a conflict or ask for advice on a situation they feel could have been handled better. Use these experiences to refine your own skills.

Conflict Resolution Skills

Situation Involving Conflict	What You Did to Resolve It	What Else Could Have Been Done?
1.		
2.		
3.		

Negative Communication Element No. 3:   Carelessness

With all we do each day, it is understandable that sometimes we neglect to devote our full attention to the task at hand. However, when you work in child care, you are responsible, not just for your own well-being, but also for the well-being of the children who depend on you. In order to be an effective communicator, you must also be organized. With numerous children in your care and many different activities occurring on a regular basis, you need to find a system to effectively communicate happenings to the families. Methods such as newsletters, bulletin boards, and other current event notices will be discussed in Chapters 6 and 7. The important message is not which method you choose, but that you must be careful to keep the information current and easily accessible to all families. Small oversights can turn into major misunderstandings if you are not adequately prepared to disseminate information.

In this situation, carelessness resulted in hurt feelings for a child and her family. Child care providers need to be acutely aware that almost all of their actions affect the children they care for. Poor planning or judgment will ultimately have adverse

WHEN COMMUNICATION BREAKS DOWN

A teacher uses notices in classroom mailboxes as his method of informing families when special events are occurring in his class. Tuesday was planned to be a special Tie-Dye Day, and all of the children needed to bring in white shirts from home. The teacher had been extremely busy during the previous week and did not have an opportunity to place the note about the upcoming event into the children's mailboxes until Monday, the day before the project. One child was absent on Monday, and therefore the family never received the notice. When it came time for the special tie-dye project, the child did not have the needed shirt and the teacher had neglected to bring any extras. Through no fault of her own, the child simply had to watch the other children have fun during the project. She was not able to participate and felt very left out. The family understandably became upset at pickup time when their child was the only one not proudly displaying a tie-dye creation.

EFFECTIVE COMMUNICATION IN ACTION

A teacher sees from his lesson plan that Tie-Dye Day, which happens to be one of the children's favorite activities, is coming up in two weeks. The families have already been notified of this in the monthly newsletter, but he knows that this may have been overlooked by some. The teacher places a note in the mailbox of each child a week before the activity. The note requests that children bring a plain shirt to school and asks that they arrive at school in old play clothes, in the event the dye ends up on the child in addition to the shirt. The day before the activity, the teacher places another reminder on the bulletin board immediately inside the classroom door. He also tries to verbally remind each family at pickup time. In the event that some families neglect to bring a shirt for the child, the teacher brings in several extras.

OUTCOME: The teacher planned ahead. He communicated with the families using several methods, and all children were able to participate because all of the parents were well informed of the activity.

consequences for the children. When you have this much responsibility, you need to ensure that you carefully plan all of your activities. Some of the most effective teachers plan out the day's lesson weeks in advance. This allows ample time to ensure you have the correct materials on hand and to notify families of any additional preparation on their part.

With each communication, you build your reputation. This is why it is so crucial to ensure that your message is received and understood by your audience. By communicating with your audience in a way that is *clear, consistent,* and *caring,* you are projecting that you are a professional who can be trusted. A family is unlikely to leave a child in your care if they do not feel at ease with the way you conduct yourself. Your trustworthiness may be called into question if you allow the elements of *confrontation, conflict,* or *carelessness* to creep into your communications. You should strive to incorporate the three positive C's and eliminate the three negative C's in each communication. If you make positive interactions a part of your everyday routine, you will strengthen your relationships with all five of your target audiences.

Communication Progress Report

Skill or Task	Range of Abilities		
	ALMOST ALWAYS	EMERGING SKILL	WILL LEARN
I can identity the three positive communication C's.	☐	☐	☐
I can identify the three negative communication C's.	☐	☐	☐
Discussions with families are clear and jargon free.	☐	☐	☐
Ample time is allowed for any questions or clarifications following communication.	☐	☐	☐
The policies and procedures of the center are consistently implemented.	☐	☐	☐
The main concern of all communications focuses around what is best for the children enrolled in the center.	☐	☐	☐
Appropriate body language is used to demonstrate the importance of each communication.	☐	☐	☐
I can control emotions and maintain a professional level of communication during difficult situations.	☐	☐	☐
I can accept viewpoints that differ from my own in a nonjudgmental manner.	☐	☐	☐
All activities are carefully planned and families are given ample advance notice.	☐	☐	☐

Essential Communication Skills in Staff Training

COMING ATTRACTIONS

- How to design an employee handbook that effectively introduces the center to new staff members

- How to effectively evaluate, review, and provide feedback to your staff

- How to hold effective staff meetings

Your staff has a tremendous amount of influence on the success of your business. Families may come to equate their child's teacher with the center. It is very important that the association be a positive one. The process of training your staff should be continuous and constantly evolving. Your staff members are as unique as the children they teach. In order for your center to run smoothly and harmoniously, you need to harness the individual experiences and talents that each one of your teachers can contribute.

Starting a new job is exciting, but can at times be overwhelming. An employee handbook is a useful tool for helping new staff members get acquainted with the center and what will be expected of them in their new position. The employee handbook should explain personnel policies and benefits as well as specific opportunities and responsibilities. Your staff handbook can be divided into five separate sections: General Operations, On the Job, Center Policies, Benefits, and Time Away from Work.

General Operations

The first section of your employee handbook should govern **general operations** and include summaries of some of the legal rights of your employees. It should be noted from the outset that the employee handbook is for informational purposes only and cannot be viewed as a contract. Most centers adhere to the policy of employment-at-will, which permits the corporation or the employee to terminate the employment relationship at any time, for any reason. If your center adheres to this policy, you should have a statement saying so in your employee handbook. You should also state that although the employee handbook summarizes the current benefit plans, it does not guarantee any continuation of benefits.

The General Operations section of the employee handbook should also contain statements on the center's compliance with equal opportunity employment. If your center has 15 or more full-time employees, it is federal law that you comply with Title VII of the Civil Rights Act of 1964, which prohibits discrimination against race, color, religion, sex, or national origin, and Title I of the Americans with Disabilities Act of 1990 (ADA), which prohibits employment discrimination against qualified individuals with disabilities. If your business employs 20 or more individuals, you must also be compliant with the Age Discrimination in Employment Act of 1967 (ADEA), which prohibits age discrimination against individuals who are 40 years of age or older. The number of employees includes full-time, part-time, and temporary staff members. All businesses with one or more employees must abide by the Equal Pay Act of 1963 (EPA), which prohibits wage discrimination between men and women in substantially equal jobs within the same establishment. If these laws are applicable to your center, you should include this information in your handbook along with statements assuring your compliance with these federal regulations. The U.S. Equal Employment Opportunity Commission (EEOC) should be consulted regarding any questions you may have about the applicablility of these laws to your center. The EEOC has designated a special department as a resource for small business owners. You can access this information on-line at http://www.eeoc.gov. The EEOC also provides workshops tailored for the small business owner who may not have a specialized human resources department to handle the legal issues surrounding the employer-employee relationship.

On the Job

The next section of your employee handbook should address what your employees can expect while they are on the job. As your center continues to grow, this section will develop based on your experiences. It should address questions which may arise during the course of a normal workday. Some issues that should be given consideration in the On the Job section are the following:

- introductory period
- new employee orientation
- employee suggestions and ideas
- communication with management
- recording work time
- paychecks
- performance reviews
- promotions and pay raises
- definition of the workweek
- meal breaks
- planning time
- personal telephone calls

Introductory period. Does your center have a set period of time in which employees and employers can determine if a suitable match has been made? Many centers have an introductory period of three months, ending in an evaluation.

New employee orientation. What type of formal orientation does your center offer? At a mininum, you should require employees to read the handbook and to sign a statement stating they have reviewed and understand the statements contained within it. Your center may find it useful to put together a checklist to formally document training.

ACTIVITY 3.1 Designing a New Teacher Orientation Checklist

Customize the template provided on page 34 to design an orientation checklist that fits the needs of your center.

New Teacher Orientation Checklist Template

Print this form from the enclosed CD!

Name:		Employee No:
Position:		Starting Date:

Item	Employee Initials & Date	Supervisor Initials & Date
Program Philosophy		
Tour of Center		
Located the: First Aid Box		
Fire Evacuation Plans		
Staff & Children's Bathrooms		
Staff Storage		
Time Clock/Sign-In Sheets		
Staff Information Board		
Staff Mailbox		
Kitchen/Baking Procedures		
Where to Park		
Reference Books		
Curriculum Books & Files		
Equipment		
Rec'd. & Read: Job Description		
Personnel Policies		
Parent Handbook/Staff		
Confidentiality Policy		
Babysitting Policy		
Dress Code		
Reviewed: Health Checks		
Infection Control		
Hand Washing		
Attendance Record Keeping		
Sign-In Book		
Discipline Policy		
Playground & Safety Procedures		
Fire Alarm/Evacuation		
First Aid/Accident Procedure		
Medication Procedure		
Child Abuse Reporting Procedure		
Class Management		

New Teacher Orientation Checklist Template *(Continued)*

Item		Employee Initials & Date	Supervisor Initials & Date
	Mailbox/Cubbies		
	Bulletin Boards		
	Snack Calendar		
	Naptime Procedures		
	Free Choice		
	Calendar Time		
	Parent Info. Board		
	Field Trip Procedure & Attire		
	Special Events		
	Coming Attractions/Lesson Plans		
	Staff Biography		
	Receipt Page of Handbook		
	Payday/Hours/Breaks		
	Time Off/Benefits		
Completed:	New Employee Form		

Employee suggestions and ideas. Does your center have a process for accepting suggestions from your employees? Is there a suggestion box or a regular meeting that could accommodate employee suggestions? Even if it is not feasible to put all of the ideas into practice, most employees enjoy having a forum for their comments.

Communication with management. How should your employees voice problems, questions, or complaints? The accumulation of unspoken or unanswered issues can be detrimental to the working relationship. Does the management of your center have an open door policy? An open door policy lets your staff know that all matters of conflict should be immediately brought to the attention of the appropriate supervisor for discussion.

Recording work time. Do you have a formal system for maintaining an accurate record of time worked? Are employees required to maintain these records or will they be maintained by the management of the center?

Paychecks. When can employees expect their paychecks (weekly, biweekly)? When the payday falls on a holiday, can employees expect to be paid on the last working day before the holiday or the first working day after the holiday?

Performance reviews. How often can employees expect a formal review? What will be involved in the review? Different types of reviews and other staff evaluations will be discussed in detail later in the chapter.

Promotions and pay raises. Does your center seek to promote qualified current employees to new or vacated positions? Are pay raises guaranteed on an annual basis or are they dependent on performance? Does the profitability of the corporation have an effect on pay raises?

Definition of the workweek. What are the normal business hours of the center? Will your staff have a rotating schedule or will their hours be fixed? Will employees ever be required to work weekends or evenings? Will overtime ever be needed? If so, must this be approved by a supervisor in advance?

Meal breaks. How much time off will each employee be given? Will this be paid or unpaid? You should check state labor laws to ensure you are in compliance.

Planning time. Will your staff be provided with planning time each week? If so, how will this be scheduled, and are staff required to remain on-site?

Personal telephone calls. Is use of the center phone permitted for staff members? How will messages be relayed to the staff members. Will staff be notified promptly of personal emergencies? Does your center permit the staff to place or receive cell phone calls while in the classroom?

Center Policies

In addition to the everyday procedures discussed in the On the Job section of the staff handbook, you also need to make new members to your team aware of broader guidelines that relate to their conduct at the center. In the section entitled Center Policies, you should provide readers with some basic information on the ethical principles with which they are expected to abide as representatives of the center. Your Center Policies section should give consideration to the following:

- confidentiality of family matters
- care of children's records
- attendance and punctuality
- standards of conduct
- care of equipment
- dress code
- outside employment
- substance abuse

Confidentiality of family matters. As a child care provider, many families provide you with a privileged glimpse into their personal lives. In order to maintain a professional standing in the community, you need to ensure that your staff respects the confidentiality of any personal information to which they may have access. You can impress this responsibility upon your staff by including a statement in the staff handbook that stresses the need for confidentiality and provides for disciplinary action if confidentiality is violated. The following is a general confidentiality statement.

> Professional ethics require that each employee maintain the highest degree of confidentiality when handling family and children affairs. In order to maintain this professional confidence, no employee shall disclose family or children information to outsiders. Violation of this policy will result in disciplinary action, up to and including termination.

Care of children's records. The impression that families have of your corporation will be partly based on how you care for their records. Centers that are careless with files and records give families the impression that the same attitude may be directed toward care of their children in the classroom. It is the professional duty of your staff members to respect the confidence placed in them by ensuring that children's files are handled with care. When possible, your personnel should view material in the files and take notes rather than removing material from the file. It is standard procedure at most centers to prohibit the removal of records or files from the center premises.

Attendance and punctuality. The child care center only functions properly when your staff members are able to work as a cohesive team. This requires that each person be in the right place at the right time. How should employees notify the center if they are going to be late or absent from work? Do you have a maximum number of days an employee can be absent without proper notification of the center before you consider the job to be abandoned? How will employees who are chronically late or absent be disciplined?

Standards of conduct. Each of your employees has an obligation to observe and follow the policies of the center. Proper standards of conduct must be maintained at all times. Corrective disciplinary actions must be taken if an individual's behavior interferes with the orderly and efficient operation of the center. You should outline the hierarchy of disciplinary actions. The typical progression is verbal warning, written warning, suspension without pay, and discharge. However, you should note in this section that one form of action will not necessarily precede another. It may also be useful to provide a list of what actions may result in disciplinary procedures, including discharge. The following is a standard, but not exhaustive, list of actions that require disciplinary intervention:

1. physical or verbal mistreatment of children
2. child endangerment
3. violation of the corporation's policies or safety rules
4. abusive or inconsiderate treatment of coworkers, families, or visitors
5. insubordination, that is, refusal to perform assigned work or follow instructions
6. poor attendance
7. possession, use, or sale of alcohol or a controlled substance on work premises or during work hours
8. unauthorized possession, use, or sale of weapons, including firearms, or explosives on work premises

9. theft or dishonesty

10. physical harassment, sexual harassment, or disrespect toward coworkers, visitors, or other members of the public

11. poor performance

12. sleeping during work hours

Care of equipment. You have invested a great deal to provide the equipment your center needs to function. Your staff can help you minimize wear and tear by ensuring that proper care is always used when utilizing company equipment. All lost or broken equipment should be reported to a supervisor, and property should not be removed from the center.

Dress code. In order to maintain a professional appearance, you may want to consider a center dress code. A properly attired individual helps to create a favorable image for the center. Whether or not a staff member's job responsibility involves direct contact with families, each staff member represents your center in appearance as well as actions. When designing your dress code policy, you should also take into consideration that the dress code at a child care center will have to be more relaxed than the typical dress code of other businesses, given the physical and often messy nature of the job. Some centers also choose to have more relaxed dress codes in the summer months, when learning takes a less structured approach.

Outside employment. Some of your staff may find it necessary to seek additional employment outside of the center. It is important that outside employment not conflict with the staff member's responsibilities at the center. You may want to consider asking your staff to notify the center's management in writing if they choose to accept an outside position. It is generally not advisable for any staff members to also be employed by a competitor.

Substance abuse. The responsibility of caring for children is one that demands absolute clarity of mind. As such, many centers find it is important to take a no-exceptions approach to substance use while at work or on center premises. Full compliance with a substance abuse policy should be a condition of hiring and of continued employment.

Benefits

The fourth section of your handbook should provide your employees with information about the **benefits** your center offers. Specifics about benefit plans may need to be addressed in stand-alone documents, as these can change from year to year. However, an overview on the types of benefits available is a useful tool for new employees. The type of benefits your center offers will be dependent on the size of your employee pool, but the benefit section typically covers the following:

- holidays
- vacation
- sick/personal days

- medical insurance
- COBRA
- 401(k)
- workers' compensation
- bonus plan
- professional development

Holidays. How many holidays are observed by your center annually? It is not advised to list the specific days in the handbook, as these may be variable depending on the year. When are full-time employees eligible for paid holidays (upon hiring or after completing the introductory period)? Are part-time employees eligible for paid holidays? Are staff members permitted to take a vacation day either the day before or after a holiday?

Vacation. How many paid vacation days are given per year? When are employees eligible for paid vacation? Does the number of paid vacation days increase according to yearly anniversary dates? How should employees notify the management of their intended vacation days? Can unused vacation days be carried over to the next year? Upon voluntary or involuntary termination, will employees be paid for any earned but unused vacation time?

Sick or personal days. How many days are permitted per year for sick or personal days? How should employees notify the management of intended personal days? Can unused sick or personal days be carried over to the next year? Will employees be paid for any unused sick or personal time upon voluntary or involuntary termination?

Medical insurance. Is medical insurance offered as a benefit to your employees? Does the center provide assistance to employees with some portion of the cost? Who is eligible to participate in the plan? Specifics of the plan should not be discussed in the handbook, as this information can change annually. Separate information packets or booklets should be provided by the insurance carrier as a supplement to the information given in the handbook.

Consolidated Omnibus Budget Reconciliation Act (COBRA). Under federal law, most employers who sponsor group medical or dental insurance are required to offer the opportunity for a temporary extension in instances where the coverage would otherwise end. Under COBRA, staff members who would normally lose their insurance due to a decrease in hours or termination of employment may elect to continue coverage for up to 36 months. The staff member electing COBRA insurance is responsible for paying the insurance premiums at the group rate.

401(k). Does your center maintain a 401(k) or other retirement plan? Who is eligible for participation in this plan? Details of the plan should not be included in the staff handbook but should be provided as a supplement.

Workers' compensation. On-the-job injuries must be covered by a workers' compensation insurance policy. These injuries should not be treated through medical insurance.

It is important that employees know that they are responsible for reporting all injuries, even minor ones, immediately to their supervisor.

Bonus plan. Does your center offer a merit-based bonus plan? Who is eligible for this plan and how is merit determined? Are there other factors, such as profitability, that may affect the determination of bonuses?

Professional development. One of the most important benefits you can offer your staff is the opportunity to continue development of their skills. There are a wide variety of educational programs and seminars focused on the child care professional. Will your center reimburse staff members for the cost of continuing professional education?

Time Away from Work

Life can be unpredictable, but as a child care professional you need to have a plan in place to cope with the unexpected. In the Time Away from Work section, you should let your staff members know what they can expect if they find it necessary to take a prolonged absence from their duties. The following scenarios should be addressed in this section: Jury Duty, Bereavement, Leave of Absence, Pregnancy, and Severe Weather. There are likely to be state and federal laws governing some of these situations. It is a good idea to have an attorney review your handbook prior to printing to ensure that you are in compliance with all legal issues.

You should allow your new staff member ample time to read the staff handbook and ask any questions that may arise. The staff handbook can only address general corporate issues. You will also need to provide more specific information and training related to the actual job description of the new employee. It is a good idea to compile a comprehensive job description for each position in your center. This job description should be reviewed with the new employee during the training period. You should ensure that the new staff member understands each line of the job description and what will be expected. By communicating your expections at the outset, you are less likely to encounter confusion and frustration at a later date. You should be sure to incorporate the three positive C's (clarity, consistency, and caring) into your job descriptions. The job descriptions can also be modified for use during evaluations. If you have thoroughly discussed expectations with the new employee, there should be no surprises during the review, when evaluation will be done on the same parameters.

ACTIVITY 3.2 Designing a Teacher Job Description

Customize the template provided on page 41 to design a comprehensive job description for new teachers.

Teacher Job Description Template

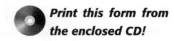
Print this form from the enclosed CD!

Basic Function:

To provide a warm, nurturing, safe, and loving environment for [center] students, while guiding them through age-appropriate activities to foster a sense of self-esteem and a love of discovery and learning.

A. Program Skills/Abilities

1. Thinks quickly and logically under normal situations and under pressure.

2. Understands all phases of assigned duties and completes tasks with little supervision.

3. Is well prepared for class, has materials ready in advance.

4. _____

5. _____

6. _____

7. _____

8. _____

9. _____

10. _____

B. Child Interaction and Instructional Skills

1. Uses a variety of teaching strategies to enhance children's learning and development.

2. Interacts with the children and encourages their involvement in activities.

3. Demonstrates creativity and resourcefulness in planning age-appropriate activities.

4. _____

5. _____

6. _____

7. _____

8. _____

9. _____

10. _____

C. Parent Interaction

1. Establishes and maintains good daily communications with parents, speaking with them in a positive, courteous manner.

2. Remains sensitive to the needs of parents.

(Continued)

Teacher Job Description Template *(Continued)*

3. Supports cultural differences and avoids favoritism.

4. _____

5. _____

6. _____

7. _____

8. _____

9. _____

10. _____

D. Staff Interaction

1. Assists others when time allows.

2. Seeks out new and better ways of doing tasks.

3. Exhibits flexibility by changing plans in order to meet deadlines.

4. _____

5. _____

6. _____

7. _____

8. _____

9. _____

10. _____

Skills: Well-developed written and verbal skills

Knowledge of child development

Understanding of appropriate child-teacher and family-teacher relations and interactions

Diplomacy

Strong organizational and planning skills

High degree of professionalism

Physical ability as required to perform duties

Education/Training: College degree in early childhood education or child-related field

Experience: Prior teaching experience is desirable

Position Reports to: Head Teacher

When the job is as hands-on as teaching, there is only so much that can be described on paper. Caring for children is definitely a responsibility where you learn best by doing. It is recommended that your new staff members be given the opportunity to "shadow" current teachers. Depending on the amount of time you have before the new staff member must assume his or her individual responsibilities, the shadowing could last anywhere from a few hours to a week. If time permits, it is useful to have the new staff member shadow several different people, even those with a different job description. A team functions best when everyone understands and respects the roles of all of the team members.

It is the responsibility of the center director to introduce the new staff member to the existing team. If you are unavailable, you should designate this responsibility to a senior member of your team. Some new employees have a difficult time introducing themselves to others, so you should make the transition easier for them by facilitating the introductions. You want your new employees to feel at ease at your center.

Once your new staff member has fully assumed all responsibilities, you should continue to make yourself available for questions and to provide guidance. It is common for situations to arise that were not discussed during the introductory period. If your staff is ever unsure about how to handle a situation, they should feel that they are able to turn to a more senior member of the center for guidance. If your center has an open door policy, this should be stressed during the training period. It is much easier to answer a question than it is to rectify a situation that has been incorrectly handled. It is also a good policy to periodically check in with your new staff members to see how they think they are adjusting to the new position. Keep the lines of communication open so slight misunderstandings do not snowball.

Most centers utilize some type of formal review process. This process should be summarized in your staff handbook so your employees know how frequently they can expect feedback on their performance. The review process should be structured so it serves as a learning opportunity rather than simply a list of what has been done right or wrong over the previous observation period. If you put together a comprehensive job description (see Activity 3.2), you can adapt the same document to use for performance evaluation.

ACTIVITY 3.3 Designing a Teacher Performance Evaluation

Customize the template provided on page 44 to design a comprehensive performance evaluation for your teachers. The items on which staff members are evaluated should mimic the items in their job description. You cannot fairly evaluate employees on tasks they were unaware of being responsible for.

Print this form from the enclosed CD!

Teacher Performance Evaluation Template

Basic Function:

The purpose of this evaluation is to serve as a helpful tool to assess job performance.

Your performance is rated on a scale of 1 to 5.

1. = poor performance, rarely meets expectations

2. = average performance, sometimes does not meet expectations

3. = good performance, meets all expectations

4. = excellent performance, sometimes exceeds expectations

5. = exemplary performance, consistently exceeds expectations

Staff name: _____   Date: _____

A. Program Skills/Abilities

1. Thinks quickly and logically under normal situations and under pressure.

2. Understands all phases of assigned duties and completes tasks with little supervision.

3. Is well prepared for class, has materials ready in advance.

4. _____

5. _____

6. _____

7. _____

B. Child Interaction & Instructional Skills

1. Uses a variety of teaching strategies to enhance children's learning and development.

2. Interacts with the children and encourages their involvement in activities.

3. Demonstrates creativity and resourcefulness in planning age-appropriate activities.

4. _____

5. _____

6. _____

7. _____

C. Parent Interaction

1. Establishes and maintains good daily communications with parents, speaking to them in a positive, courteous manner.

2. Remains sensitive to the needs of parents.

Teacher Performance Evaluation Template *(Continued)*

3. Supports cultural differences and avoids favoritism.

4. _____

5. _____

6. _____

7. _____

D. Staff Interaction

1. Assists others when time allows.

2. Seeks out new and better ways of doing tasks.

3. Exhibits flexibility by changing plans in order to meet deadlines.

4. _____

5. _____

6. _____

7. _____

Exemplary performance rating	300–270 points = 8% raise
Excellent performance rating	269–240 points = 5% raise
Good performance rating	239–180 points = 4% raise
Average performance rating	179–120 points = 3% raise
Unacceptable performance	Less than 120

Employee's additional comments:

_____

_____

_____

_____

Supervisor's additional comments:

_____

_____

_____

_____

_____

_____   _____
Employee signature   Supervisor signature

The evaluation should be completed by the most senior person who has regular, direct contact with the employee. It can be difficult for employees to value an assessment performed by an individual with whom they have had limited interaction. The manager should complete the evaluation based on the employee's overall performance; an isolated event should not dominate the entire review. Although it is much easier said than done, evaluations should not be colored by personal opinions or attitudes. It is the responsibility of the manager to review the employee based on observed interactions with the children, families, and other staff members, in addition to the manager's own experience with the employee. It is human nature to become nervous when you know your actions are being scrutinized, so in order to obtain a clear picture of the employee's everday performance, the manager should strive to perform evaluations in as nonintrusive a manner as possible.

Evaluations are extremely important to both your center and your employees, so they should be scheduled as any other important conference would be. Arrange time in advance so the employee and manager can sit down and review the evaluation document together. The environment should be a quiet and private one as confidential information will be discussed. Make sure you schedule plenty of time, as the employee will likely have questions. When communicating the performance review to the employee you should avoid elements of the three negative C's (confrontation, conflict, and carelessness). The meeting and evaluation document should be structured so the environment is one of learning, not criticism. If a staff member receives a low performance rating, you should be prepared to back up the score with specific examples. You should also be able to offer constructive advice on how this area can be improved for the future. There may be an issue that you and the employee being reviewed see differently. If so, the employee should have some means of disputing the area of conflict. In the template provided in Activity 3.3, there is an area for employee comments, where employees who feel that they have been unjustly reviewed can add their justification to the evaluation findings.

If your center experiences a serious breach of its policies, the issue should be addressed immediately. Depending on the severity, the incident should be acknowledged through either a verbal or written warning, as outlined in the Standards of Conduct page of the Center Policies section. Verbal warnings should be discussed in a calm and nonconfrontational manner. The setting should be a quiet and private area where both parties can sit down and review the situation. Out of respect for your employees, anyone who is not directly impacted by the situation should not be made aware of the verbal warning. Everyone makes mistakes, and your staff members should have the opportunity to correct their actions without being subjected to the additional scrutiny of others.

All serious breaches of conduct, especially if child safety has been compromised, should be documented by a written warning. If the staff member is ultimately terminated, the written documentation will help to protect you and the center in the unlikely event a lawsuit is filed. If you did not directly witness the incident in question, you should obtain as much information as you can from all parties involved. Before you commit the situation to paper, it is your responsibility to ensure that you have a clear picture of what actually transpired. A meeting should be arranged to discuss the situation and to present the employee with the written warning. The warning should be structured in such a way that the employee is clear on what specific event has caused the written warning. The employee should also understand why the behavior is unacceptable in the center, how the center recommends the actions be corrected, and the consequences of neglecting the recommendations. Moreover, the written warning should state the time frame in which the employee must implement the center's corrective plan of action. It is important that you be consistent when issuing verbal or written warnings. An action that results in a verbal warning for one staff member should not result in a written warning for another.

Since you have multiple opportunities to evaluate your staff, you may want to consider allowing them the same opportunity to evaluate the center management. Completion of an anyomous survey can give you some candid answers regarding the job satisfaction of your employees. Turnover rates can be high in the child care field. The proper training of new employees requires a great deal of time, and your families may feel anxiety about frequent changes in their child's classroom. It is to your advantage to retain your high-performing staff members. By allowing your staff to evaluate the management, you are providing them with an outlet for any frustrations they may not otherwise be able to communicate. An evaluation can also serve as a learning experience for you, allowing you to see how your communication and managerial techniques are received by your employees.

Too often, performance reviews carry a negative connotation. Your employees deserve to be recognized for their positive contributions to the center. This can be facilitated by providing your families with a forum to recognize a job well done. It is amazing how a simple note of thanks can really brighten someone's day. Caring for children is a job that is both emotionally and physically demanding, so it is important for staff to know that their efforts are noticed and appreciated. Your staff members will need to feel valued in order to continue doing a good job.

ACTIVITY 3.4 Designing a Staff Feedback Evaluation

Customize the template provided on page 48 to design an evaluation that your staff members can use to communicate their feelings about the management of the center. Since your employees will be commenting on their supervisors, this form should be voluntary and anonymous.

ACTIVITY 3.5 Designing a Family Feedback Evaluation

Customize the template provided on page 49 to design a form your families can use to express their thanks for their favorite staff member. You can keep these forms in a place that is easily accessible to all of your families.

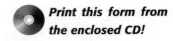
Print this form from the enclosed CD!

Staff Feedback Evaluation Template

Does the director foster a positive work environment?   Y   N

Does the director communicate clearly defined expectations?   Y   N

Does the director support cooperation and team efforts?   Y   N

Does the director respond to staff questions and concerns?   Y   N

Does the director communicate the mission to staff and families?   Y   N

Does the director effectively oversee program operations?   Y   N

Does the director keep abreast of program issues as they arise?   Y   N

Do you enjoy your work? If not, what can be done to help you enjoy your work? _____

_____

_____

Do you feel your views, suggestions, and concerns are taken seriously? If not, what can be done to improve this

situation? _____

_____

_____

Are there any policies that are unclear, unfair, or need to be changed? _____

_____

_____

If you were the director of the center, what changes would you make and why? _____

_____

_____

What can be done to facilitate better communication between the director and staff? _____

_____

_____

What can be done to improve working conditions at the center? _____

_____

_____

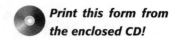
Print this form from the enclosed CD!

Family Feedback Evaluation Template

Please check (✓) the following position your family would like to recognize:

☐ Owner/Executive Director

☐ Director

☐ Office Manager

☐ Assistant Director

☐ Head Teacher

☐ Teacher

☐ Nurse

☐ Teacher Assistant

Our family _____

(Family name)

would like to recognize _____

(Staff name)

for doing an excellent job!

Comments: _____

_____

_____

_____

_____

_____

_____

_____

Thank you! Please drop the form in the office.

Planned communication with your staff members does not cease at the conclusion of the orientation period. Staff members who feel informed, valued, and integral to the success of the school will represent themselves and the school in a positive manner. Regular staff meetings are an effective method for both ensuring that your staff is well informed and providing an avenue for staff members to become involved in decisions important to the functioning of the center. The content of the staff meeting will be dependent on the goal of the session. There are typically three types of staff meetings; annual meetings, monthly meetings, and weekly meetings.

When people feel as though they have no voice, it is easy for them to become overwhelmed. The child care profession is full of people who have been led down the path to burnout. The workload becomes overwhelming, and help is nowhere in sight. No one seems to have a clue as to what needs to be done. In other words, there is no leadership. How a director and other program administrators set the tone can make the difference between success and failure of a center. The main objective of each of your staff meetings, whether annual, monthly, or weekly, is to provide some direction for your staff. Attendees should leave your meetings feeling as though they have a clearer picture of what lies ahead. This understanding can decrease anxiety and feelings of being overwhelmed. If you have a staff member who feels that the workload is too cumbersome, regular staff meetings also provide an outlet for that person to ask for help or seek advice from others in the same situation. Regular communication can address a problem before it spirals out of control.

As in any organization, the leader cannot be available 100 percent of the time. The staff needs to be trained and informed how to act in the best interest of the children and the school. The objective of a yearly staff meeting is to establish the plans and goals for the year. At the conclusion of this meeting, your staff should feel comfortable in discussing these plans with your families. The initial planning for the year is usually the responsibility of the administrator or director. The administrators take on the job of being the visionary. They are responsible for forecasting trends in the community and designing plans to meet its child care needs. Not only should administrators set forth future goals, but they should also ask their staff to work with them and include their areas of expertise. The yearly staff meeting provides the director with an opportunity to share these plans with the other staff members, receive feedback, and collaboratively make any needed change. This interactive process will encourage all staff members to become involved with and committed to their programs. Since this meeting will cover many different topics, it is important to prepare an outline in advance of the actual meeting. While preparation of the outline is director responsibility, staff members should be encouraged to offer any topics they feel would be beneficial to discuss.

ACTIVITY 3.6 Designing a Yearly Staff Meeting Agenda

Using the template provided on page 51, create an agenda that address the important points to be discussed at a yearly staff meeting. Discussion topics should include policies and procedures as well as opportunities for staff members to contribute to the development of the center materials and programs.

Yearly Staff Meeting Agenda Template

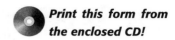

Print this form from the enclosed CD!

Purpose: Inform staff of new and existing policies and procedures. Implement staff and family suggestions and discuss issues pertaining to school.

Welcome and Introduction of Staff

Staff Meeting: Weekly—Individual classrooms
Monthly—Programs
Yearly—Entire Staff

Our Purpose/Mission

Our Philosophy

Staff: Code of ethics
Promoting a positive work environment
Communication/problem solving, decision making, solutions
Professional
Job description

Staff Responsibilities: Supervision of children, playground interaction, and class management, role-modeling, patience, use equipment and toys properly, clean and orderly classrooms, notification of absences, time off

Children: Age appropriateness, developing self-esteem, emotional growth, positive discipline, redirection, guidance, acceptance, understanding

Child Assessments: One-month initial observation, fall written assessment, yearly parent-teacher conferences, additional ideas from the staff

Families: Security, comfort, communication, complaints, or concerns; open door

Policy & Procedures: Staff Handbooks, Parent Handbook, Confidentiality Policy, Babysitting Policy, name tags, dress code, parking

Health & Safety: Sick Policy, Medical Emergencies Policy, First-Aid Policy, injuries, allergies, Evacuation Policy, fire drill, inclement weather

Bathroom: Open doors, monitoring, hand washing

Personnel File: What is included, reviews, evaluations, compensation and bonus plan

Front Office: Privacy requested for meetings, administration equipment

Staff Lounge: Telephone, TV, refrigerator, copy machine, laminator, time sheets, information board, resources, mailboxes

Community Involvement: Community outreach, fundraising, senior interaction, literacy council

National Organizations: Mission, goals, accreditation procedures, how you can become involved

Child Drop-off & Pickup: Sign-in and -out procedure, late pickup forms, fees, proper identification, no pickup by siblings under age 16 years

Development of New Activities, Curriculum, Materials: What would you like to see added or changed?

Questions and Comments:

In order to achieve all of the goals set forth at the annual staff meetings, you will need to keep the lines of communication open. This will require the director or head teacher to break down and organize the top priorities for each program. These issues will be the topic of discussion at monthly staff meetings.

Monthly staff meetings will outline what each individual will be responsible for contributing during the upcoming month. The staff should be given opportunities to volunteer for the various tasks. A director who is well informed can assign duties to the person with the most experience or knowledge in each of the needed areas. For example, the cooking project may be assigned to a person who enjoys cooking or simply to the person who lives close to a food discount center. The most important factor in all of these meetings is the communication. It is the responsibility of the director to encourage all staff members to become involved and interested in contributing to the success of the center. Establishing clear lines of communication is a shared responsibility of all members of the staff. It is impractical to designate one person to "spread the word." Good communication networks are built from the ground up; you can only achieve effective communication when every employee is involved. Monthly staff meetings will encourage this type of communication and will allow your staff members to work together as a group to accomplish their goals.

ACTIVITY 3.7 Designing a Monthly Staff Meeting Agenda

Using the template provided on page 53, create an agenda that address the important points to be discussed at a monthly staff meeting. Discussion topics should include upcoming curriculum activities as well as opportunities for staff members to continue their own professional development.

Some centers have also found value in scheduling **weekly staff meetings.** These meetings will outline the day-to-day activities for the upcoming week. Unfortunately, most centers are not able to release teachers every week to attend a staff meeting. These meetings usually are done at the end of the day or before school starts. If a weekly staff meeting is an imperative at your center you can consider asking the staff to use one of their lunches a week to hold their meetings. The weekly meeting can offer a wide range of benefits. It gives the teachers time to think as a team. It allows the opportunity to benefit from the expertise of one another. Providing your staff with this open door of communication and information will only enhance their sense of commitment to their own standards of performance.

Monthly Staff Meeting and Agenda Template

Print this form from the enclosed CD!

Monthly Theme: _____

Monthly Readiness Skill: _____

Curriculum: Age appropriate, with hands-on learning experience including weekly themes, readiness skills, science, life skills, social skills, motor development, art, and music

Lesson Plans & Coming Attractions: Reviewed and approved two weeks in advance by head teacher. Lesson plans should be:

> well written
>
> informative
>
> age appropriate
>
> friendly
>
> neat
>
> grammatically correct

Music, movement, process art, free expression art, bulletin board displays, finger plays, puppets, stories, games, manipulatives, blocks, and dramatic play are to be included in weekly activities.

Teacher Designated Planning Time: Resources are available. All materials must remain in the center. Lesson plans are not to be done during class time. Teachers should have fun when implementing lessons.

Field Trips: Planning, scheduling, organizing, informing parents, cost, itineraries, review with staff, attire, safety, and attendance.

Special Visitors: In-house field trips enhance weekly themes or curriculum. Visitors should be included in lesson plans and Coming Attractions.

Orientations, Events, and Celebrations: Preplanned and discussed as a program. Materials, supplies, transportation arrangements, and additional needs will be based on program budget.

Monthly Classroom Observation:

Continuing Education Courses: Available workshops and classes, requirements, and criteria.

Communication Progress Report

Skill or Task	Range of Abilities		
	ALMOST ALWAYS	EMERGING SKILL	WILL LEARN
Center management are aware of and compliant with all laws governing employees.	☐	☐	☐
The staff handbook provides information on how to communicate with management.	☐	☐	☐
All new staff members complete a comprehensive orientation program.	☐	☐	☐
Expected standard of conduct is well defined in the staff handbook, as are a list of actions that will result in disciplinary measures being taken.	☐	☐	☐
Center policies are clearly stated in the staff handbook.	☐	☐	☐
Staff members have access to supplementary benefit information for items not explicitly explained in the handbook (i.e., 401k and health plans).	☐	☐	☐
A written job description has been prepared for each employee type; these are reviewed with new staff members.	☐	☐	☐
Staff members are well informed about the type and frequency of evaluations they will be receiving.	☐	☐	☐
A system is in place for staff members to receive positive feedback from families.	☐	☐	☐
Staff meetings are well organized.	☐	☐	☐
Staff members feel that the meetings are a productive use of their time.	☐	☐	☐

4

Understanding Diversity and Multiple Perspectives

COMING ATTRACTIONS

- How to convey a message of respect regarding diversity issues

- How to use role-playing as a forum for open discussion on communication challenges

- How to approach difficult situations

One of the most important skills any child care professional can possess is the ability to empathize with others. This is also one of the most difficult lessons to teach. In some cases people are not able to understand another's point of view. As teachers, we sometimes become calloused with the mistakes that we perceive parents make in the early years of child rearing. We need to stop and think why it is so easy for us to understand the behavior of children. During our careers many of us have literally cared for hundreds, if not thousands, of children. We have a lot of practice in determining what will work with children and what won't. As an early childhood educator, our job is not only to teach, but also to offer advice and guidance to both families and children in making sound judgments and decisions. We have to remember that the families and children of the center are our customers. No family *has* to go to your center. They are paying for your services. We can hope that families choose to listen to our advice, but in no sense are they required to do so.

It is also important to keep in mind that the children in your center will likely come from a wide variety of backgrounds. What you may find appropriate may nonetheless be considered completely intolerable by a family whose culture differs from yours. Communication strategies such as eye contact and shaking hands upon meeting are engrained within the culture of America but may be eschewed by other cultures. You cannot be expected to know what will be required from you by your families in order to fit their diverse needs. However, as a child care professional, you should become comfortable with discussing diversity needs with your families.

Diversity

When people speak of "diversity," they are referring to differences in color, language, gender, physical ability, financial situation, sexual orientation, and much more. Basically anything that makes up an individual's identity can be considered a part of his or her diversity. The fact that many people consider diversity issues to be those solely surrounding race is a testament to how much further our country must come to become culturally competent.

Children are aware of differences at a very young age. However, the prejudices and biases associated with differences are not innate. Play and laughter are the universal language for children's communication. The conclusion of numerous research studies regarding identity formation and attitude development is that children learn by observing the differences and similarities among people. Children are much more perceptive than they are often given credit for and, in fact, can easily absorb the spoken and unspoken messages they receive about those differences. An important part of the early classroom is learning about issues of diversity and equity. Children can simultaneously be proud of their own culture and knowledgeable and respectful of the culture of others. Your staff members should have this same attitude. Many college curriculums now incorporate issues surrounding diversity. For those who have not had formal training, cultural competency can be developed through interaction and the willingness to learn. Your center environment should feel inviting for all of your families, and your staff must be willing to learn more about their diverse needs.

The following suggestions can get you started on building an all-inclusive center.

- Avoid derogatory terms, even when the conversation is jovial.
- Don't patronize. Many families take pride in their unique backgrounds yet feel strong ties to the American culture.
- Be aware of words and gestures that others may find offensive.
- Ask your families to educate you on their backgrounds and any unique needs they may have. Use each interaction as a learning experience as you build your cultural competency. Thank your families for sharing with you.
- Ask your families to come into your center to teach the other children and teachers about their heritage. Allow the children in your center to be exposed to a variety of cultures.
- Use books and videos to bring cultures from around the world into your classroom.
- Don't overlook a child with physical or mental challenges, but at the same time, don't try to overcompensate. Allow the child and family to provide you with feedback on tasks they feel require modification.
- Ensure that the classroom is full of materials that promote diversity. Children should have a choice of skin-tone crayons, and the artwork, dolls, and other toys should reflect multiculturalism.
- Whenever you are discussing differences, be sure to emphasize that we are more alike than different.
- Immediately address any situation where a child is using racial or ethnic slurs or is negatively commenting on another's physical or academic abilities.
- Remember that you are a role model, so what you do is as important as what you say.

Role-Playing

The use of role-playing is an excellent tool for training your staff. Review the following scenarios and the accompanying discussion questions. They can provide you with valuable insight on how other people think.

ACTIVITY 4.1 Role-Playing Scenario Number 1: Janet, Jessie, and Michelle

Review the following scenario, attempting to put yourself into the shoes of the participants. Pay close attention to all of the information given before answering the questions following the scenario.

THE MOTHER: Janet is a good mother to her son, Jessie. She not only provides a nurturing environment at home, but she also maintains a full-time job. Her boss is very demanding and doesn't give much support to employees who have children. Her husband, Jim, is a good father and husband. She feels lucky to have all of this, and on most days she feels she can handle the problems that arise. However, she is also tired. Juggling both work and home is beginning to take its toll. She knows that Jim spends a lot of time commuting to and from work and that his job is very demanding. Nonetheless, Janet feels that Jim could be more helpful and take on more responsibility in running the household. She does most of the routine household chores, such as cleaning, cooking, and errands. This is done after she gets home from picking Jessie up at his day care center. Jim is always quick to help (when asked), but the nightly routine of getting Jessie fed, gathering together what he needs for his next school day, giving him a bath, and reading him a story before bedtime usually falls back into her lap.

Jessie is a good kid. He is happy and gets along with his friends at school. For the most part, he does what is asked of him and has a good temperament. Janet feels guilty about not spending more time with him. Staying home full time is not an option. Janet knows she must work in order to support the family's financial needs. Janet and Jim have discussed hiring people to help with the cleaning, but it seems to be a luxury they can't afford. The conversation always ends with Jim saying he will pitch in more to help in the future.

Janet's boss has recently been quick to point out some of the careless mistakes she has made and hint to her about the amount of commitment and work that will be needed in order for her to advance in her career.

Janet was very careful in selecting child care for her son. For the most part, she is happy with his school. The tuition cost is not insignificant, but she feels Jessie is worth it. It is important to leave her son knowing that he will be well cared for. Recently, her son was assigned to a new teacher, named Michelle. This is Jessie's third teacher. Although his teacher appears to be nice, she is very young and Janet wonders if she is qualified and how much individual attention her son really receives. She feels that for what she pays for tuition, she should see more things coming home from school and more communication from the teacher. She has been feeling this way for some time, and has decided it's time to say something to Michelle.

Michelle has recently informed her that Jessie, for no apparent reason, has occasionally hit other children. Janet is now more convinced than ever that her son's problems are due to Michelle's inexperience and lack of quality child care being given to her son. Today Michelle had requested that Janet come in early, before the normal (6:00 P.M.) pickup to discuss her son's behavior. This required Janet to ask her boss to leave work early. Her boss was unhappy with her request but let her leave anyway.

Janet managed to leave work early for the meeting but became caught in heavy traffic, so she called Jim to see if he could possibly make it in her place. It was short notice for him, and he said he was too busy to leave work. It is 6:10 when Janet finally arrives at the child care center. Not only did she miss the meeting, but she is now late for pickup. As she walks into the center, all she can think about is, "Now I'm going to pay a late fee in addition to talking about my son's behavior."

THE TEACHER: Michelle is 24 years old and has a degree in early childhood education. She always wanted to be a teacher and likes her job. She grew up in a large family and enjoys being with children. Her teaching salary is low, so there isn't much money left at the end of the month. To live on her own, she needs to share an apartment with two roommates. She needs to buy a new car and isn't sure where she will get the extra money. Nonetheless, she feels good about her life, and working with children makes her happy.

She feels lucky to have found a center that shares her philosophy. The center is well run and has a good reputation within the community. For the most part the other teachers are pleasant, and they enjoy working with each other. Turnover at the center has been high, but not as high as she has experienced at other schools. The staff has ample supplies for their classroom, and a good director runs the center. Training is provided from time to time and the parents seem to like her.

Still, this isn't what Michelle had envisioned while in college. She finds herself questioning from time to time why she doesn't have a boyfriend. The school certainly isn't a place to meet a lot of single people. Her salary is making it more difficult to afford the lifestyle she wants for herself. She envies the women who drop their children off each day. They wear nice clothes and seem to be heading off to exciting jobs. Many of the families seem to lead happily married lives.

She is dreading today. For the past few weeks, one of the children in her class, Jessie, has begun to get aggressive when playing with other children. He recently hit two other children, making them both cry. She had a difficult time in both incidences explaining the situation to the other parents. They both blamed her for not being able to manage Jessie. One parent said that the next time her child was hit, she was going to the director to complain. Michelle tried to explain that this was not normal behavior for Jessie. She has noticed that Jessie was becoming clingier with his mother in the mornings. Last week Jessie's mother had a day off from work but still brought her son to school. "If that were my child I would always keep him home on a day off," Michelle thought.

Michelle likes Jessie's mother, but she feels Janet is picking Jessie up later and later each day. This causes some resentment with Michelle because it forces her to stay late with Jessie until his mother arrives. The late fee that Michelle receives isn't worth the inconvenience. Michelle also feels that Jessie's mom looks down on child care teachers and often talks to them in a degrading manner.

Still, Michelle feels it is her responsibility to address Jessie's behavior with his mother before it gets any worse. She has some suggestions she could give her, but isn't sure if the mother will listen to any of them. She knows going into this meeting that she will have to hold her ground with this mother, who can be argumentative. Michelle has arranged to have another staff member stay with her group so she can take time with Jessie's mother.

It is now 6:10 P.M. and Jessie's mother still isn't at the center. Michelle thinks that this will also be a good opportunity to mention the lateness issue.

DISCUSSION QUESTIONS:

1. Do you think there might have been a better time to schedule this meeting?

   _____

2. Is this a good time for Michelle to discuss the lateness issue? _____

   _____

3. Is this a good time for Janet to bring up the fact she would like to see more communications from the school? _____

   _____

4. Do you think this meeting (at 6:10 P.M.) will be productive? _____

   _____

5. Does the fact that Janet and Michelle are having some communication issues affect Jessie's behavior? _____

_____

6. Is it Michelle's job to discuss late pickups or should that be the director's responsibility? _____

_____

7. How could this confrontation be avoided? _____

_____

8. What is the director's role in this situation? _____

_____

9. How can the director promote the staff as a group of respected professionals?

_____

10. Are Michelle's worries about money and lack of a boyfriend affecting her ability to relate to her students' families? _____

_____

11. Was Michelle right to wait "a few weeks" before addressing Jessie's behavior issues? _____

_____

12. Do you think the behavior issues and late pickup would be as large of an issue if Janet felt less stress at home and at work? _____

_____

13. How would you have successfully resolved this conflict? _____

_____

ACTIVITY 4.2 Role-Playing Scenario Number Two: Amy and Elizabeth

Review the following scenario, attempting to put yourself into the shoes of the participants. Pay close attention to all of the information given before answering the questions following the scenario.

THE DIRECTOR: Amy has worked at the center for the last six years. Two years ago she was promoted from head teacher to director. She is 34 years old and takes a great deal of pride in her work and the center. Amy has worked hard to earn the respect of the other employees. Many of them have an advanced degree in education, while she does not. With the school year about to begin, Amy has put in many long hours. She can often be found at the center hours after everyone else has left for the night. Amy and her husband have been hoping to start a family of their own soon, but lately Amy wonders if the demands of her job will ever allow her the opportunity to focus on her private life. Amy's husband has been upset that she has been spending so many hours at work. She can't remember the last time they sat down and had dinner together.

Tonight Amy is holding the school year kickoff meeting. All of the teachers are expected to attend. They will be presented with specific lesson plans to be followed for the first week of the new school year. Amy has created these plans based on her six years of experience at the center. She has found it most effective if all teachers introduce the program and the rules of the center in the same manner. This way, if a child has to switch classes during the year, the new routines will be similar. In addition, Amy has found that by supplying the first week's lesson plans, the teachers are much less likely to forget an important component of the children's introduction to the center. Two years ago, a new teacher had neglected to practice with her classroom what to do when they hear a fire alarm. The children were confused and terrified during the first fire drill. They did not even know which door they should line up at. Amy is determined not to let an oversight like that happen while she is in charge. Putting together the lesson plans for the first week has taken about 40 hours of Amy's time. Much of the work had to be completed at night or during the weekend. Amy is very excited to present her plans at the kickoff meeting.

Just before the meeting started, Amy received a call from Elizabeth, whom Amy had hired as a part-time teacher about six months ago. Elizabeth is well liked by many of the families and most of the other staff members. However, she has very definite ideas about how her classroom should be run. Elizabeth had told Amy that she would not be able to attend the meeting because her son was sick and she needed to stay home to be with him. This last-minute notice angers Amy, especially because she knows Elizabeth's husband works from home. Why can't he keep an eye on the sick child?

Amy sighs and lets Elizabeth know that she will be mailing her the lesson plans for the first week of school. Elizabeth promises to look them over, but before another word is said a child starts crying in the background. Elizabeth abruptly says good-bye and hangs up. Amy makes a mental note to stop by Elizabeth's classroom on the first day to make sure her plans are being followed appropriately. She considers calling Elizabeth later to give her a summary of what happened at the meeting, but then decides that, as it was Elizabeth's choice to miss the meeting, Amy should not be responsible for the extra task of bringing her up to speed. Besides, she will be mailing her the lesson plans.

THE TEACHER: Elizabeth had accepted her new position at the center about six months ago. She had previously worked full time as a head teacher for another center in the area. Elizabeth's new job means a cut in pay, responsibility, and, thankfully, hours. She is 35 years old and has two sons, ages six and eight. Elizabeth recently separated from her husband, and the children have not been taking the change well. Her oldest son has been getting in fights at school, and her youngest son has been having terrible nightmares. She is worried about the long-term impact a possible divorce would have on them. Her husband has only stopped by the house rarely since the separation, and the children miss him. She is thankful that her new job allows her to greet her children when they return from school. Her new job means that the family has to cut back on their expenses, but Elizabeth thinks the extra time together is worth having to be on a budget.

Last week Elizabeth received a phone call from Amy, the director of the center. Amy told her that she needed to come to the school year kickoff meeting, held at 6 P.M. Elizabeth was annoyed that she had so little time to arrange a sitter for her kids. She knew that many of the other teachers, Amy included, did not have the family commitments she did. Elizabeth wished she was able to attend late meetings as easily as they did, but she has her sons to think about. Still, she was excited about the school year and had a lot of great ideas she wanted to share with the group. The first week of school was Elizabeth's favorite, and she already knew exactly what activities she wanted to do with her class.

Just as Elizabeth was about to walk out the door for the meeting, her oldest son asked if she had signed him up for baseball camp yet. Elizabeth had to tell him that he would not be going to baseball camp this year; they simply could not afford it. Her son did not take this news well. He ran to the kitchen and emptied every carton of cereal they had onto the floor before running to his room and slamming the door. Elizabeth knew she could not leave a sitter in this situation, so she called Amy to let her know she was not able to make the meeting. Amy sounded annoyed, which Elizabeth expected. Just as Amy told her that she would be mailing her the curriculum for the first week, Elizabeth heard her younger son wail. His older brother had come out of his room and smacked him. Elizabeth got off the phone immediately to deal with her sons.

Elizabeth received the lesson plans in the mail two days later. She thought they were very good but also had some of her own ideas. She was sure Amy would not mind if she customized the plans; it was her classroom, after all. Elizabeth especially questioned the need to go over all of the rules of the center, including the fire drill, on the first day. She decided to move that to the second so she could use all of her enjoyable getting-to-know-you games on the first day of school. Elizabeth had found that children didn't remember much of what you taught them on the first day. It was better to save the important things until the children felt a little more comfortable at the center. Elizabeth was looking forward to the start of school.

DISCUSSION QUESTIONS:

1. How do you think the first day of school will go when Amy discovers Elizabeth is not adhering to the lesson plans? _____

_____

2. Was the conversation on the phone between Amy and Elizabeth an appropriate venue for an important discussion? _____

_____

3. How can Amy express to Elizabeth, without being confrontational, that she needs to follow Amy's lesson plans? _____

_____

4. What could Amy have done to make it clear to Elizabeth how important it was to follow her plans? _____

_____

5. Was it Elizabeth's responsibility to call Amy to get a summary of the meeting she was not able to attend or should Amy have been the one to place this call?

_____

_____

6. Are personal life and stress level impacting the job for Elizabeth? What about for Amy? _____

_____

7. How could the women work together to resolve the conflict that will inevitably occur on the first day of school? _____

_____

8. What can be done to prevent a similar situation from occurring again? _____

_____

_____

ACTIVITY 4.3 Role-Playing Scenario Number Three: Eric, Mother, and Teacher

Review the following scenario, attempting to put yourself into the shoes of the participants. Pay close attention to all of the information given before answering the questions.

THE CHILD: Today was my first day at my new school. I really didn't want to leave my other school. My best friend, Lori, was in my class there. Every Friday we could bring toys in to share, and Lori would always let me play with her toy before circle time. Since it was my very first day at this new school, my mom let me bring in my stuffed Elmo for naptime and my pirates for Show and Tell. No one wanted to play with me. All of the kids kept asking me what was wrong with my ears. I tried to hide my ears with my hat, but they would try to peak a look underneath it. I pushed one of them away, and he fell and cried. My teacher told me that I needed to learn how to be nice to my new friends. She made me go and sit on the bench. I heard my teacher tell another lady on the playground that I must have been in an accident. The other lady said that good parents are more careful with their children around fire. I don't like that other lady. She is not my real teacher and she doesn't smile. They said she was the mean teacher. When I got off the bench I decided I should just play with the balls and not the other children. I don't think I like these kids and I'm not going to play with them. At lunchtime my teacher took away my peanut butter and jelly sandwich because she said it wasn't allowed. I cried. I had to sit at a table all by myself and eat my sandwich because I wouldn't eat the cracker and cheese that they gave me. I only wanted the sandwich that my mom made me. At naptime I got my Elmo doll out of my cubby and took him to my cot. The mean lady took Elmo away from me. She said stuffed animals weren't allowed and she put him in a plastic bag. I wish it was pickup time so I could go home. I want my mom!

How would you describe Eric's first day at his new school? _____

_____

If you could make only one change in his day, what would it be? _____

_____

How might this one change impact the rest of his day? _____

_____

THE MOTHER: I arrived at my son's new school today to discover that his medical and educational records had been transferred from his old school to the director of this school. The director said she had had a lengthy conversation with the teacher from Eric's old school about some of the behavioral problems he was having in the classroom. I had hoped to discuss some of his physical limitations prior to his enrollment. There was some personal information on his records that I didn't want revealed. The director seemed to have everything under control and assured me that she had managed lots of other children with equally as bad behavioral problems and even had seen a child once with his same physical disability. She also suggested that from what she had heard from his teacher, he seemed to be showing some signs of attention-deficit hyperactivity disorder and asked if I had ever considered that as a possibility. She had even looked the disorder up on the Internet and gave me three pages of ways to test Eric at home. Since she seemed to know more than I do about the topic I decided to just leave it alone. She took me to meet his new teacher, Ms. Laura. Ms. Laura offered me one of the children's chairs to sit down in as she stood and told me all of the things she would be teaching Eric. His teacher looked familiar to me. I remembered seeing her at the restaurant the night before. She had been sitting with a group of women talking about "Katie getting bit by Jason in my class today." She had added: "There must be problems at home because he never has done anything like that before. I also heard that Jason's dad had lost his job." I was a little embarrassed that I had overheard her conversation.

As a professional, what is the single piece of advice you would give to this mother?

_____

_____

Based on this advice, how do you think the change would affect her child's learning

experience? _____

_____

Would it alter her relationship with the teacher? _____

_____

Do you feel the director was appropriate in her actions? _____

_____

THE TEACHER: The director came in last week to tell me about a new boy named Eric who would be joining my class. She gave me all of his records, so I prepared his cubby tag, added his name on the sign-out list, and posted his telephone number on the family bulletin board. I wanted to give him a jump on making arrangements for play dates with the other children. Laura told me that he was a biter, so at drop-off time I'm going to tell the other parents. I want them to be prepared for what they should expect when he comes to play at their houses. I hope the mother feels comfortable when she sees how prepared we are for his arrival. I think Laura always gives me the children with family problems. I hope she feels I am good with the bad kids. I told the other teachers during lunch in the staff room that it was their turn to have these kids in their class.

I noticed that there were a lot of blanks on Eric's transfer forms. On my class sign-in and sign-out form I left the section for the father's name blank, as there was none listed on Eric's registration form. They must have forgotten to fill in all of the blanks, so I posted it on the door and highlighted that part so I would remember to ask them when I see them. When Eric's mother stopped by the classroom today, I told her that I wouldn't be there at pickup time, but I would always let the high school aide know how Eric's day had been and she would report to her. There was a big sigh in the mother's voice when I asked her to fill in the father's name and on what days he would be dropping off.

Do you see anything wrong with the way the teacher prepared for her new student?

_____

_____

Based on what the teacher did, what do you feel will cause the most adjustment prob-

lems for Eric? _____

_____

Who is to blame for the turn of events? _____

_____

DISCUSSION QUESTIONS:

1. How was the confidentiality code violated with the mother? _____
   _____

2. How was the confidentiality code violated with the child? _____
   _____

3. Do you think there should have been a discussion between the two directors
   concerning Eric's disability prior to his enrollment? _____
   _____

4. Who should have been included in this meeting? _____
   _____

5. Do you think a conversation with Eric's classmates would have been helpful?
   _____
   _____

6. List some methods that might have eased Eric's transition to his new school.
   _____
   _____

7. How do you feel about the teacher's conversation at the restaurant? _____
   _____

8. What if the conversation happened in the staff lounge at the center? _____
   _____

9. As a director, is there anything you could do to rectify this situation? _____
   _____

10. Do you think the mother should leave her child in that school? _____
    _____

11. Explain your reasons for not moving Eric again. _____
    _____

ACTIVITY 4.4 Role-Playing Scenario Number Four: The Winter Holiday Play

Review the following scenario, attempting to put yourself into the shoes of the participants. Pay close attention to all the information given before answering the questions.

THE WINTER HOLIDAY PLAY: Each year the children practice for months in anticipation for the annual Winter Holiday play. This year the teachers decided that the children should perform "The Twelve Days of Christmas." The two weeks before the play are an especially exciting time for the children at the center. This is when the children practice their lines and families are given instructions on making the appropriate costume. Mrs. Day's class (the kindergarten class) was given the part of "5 Golden Rings." Mrs. Day was very excited because this part is one of the most exciting portions of the song and the audience always responds well. One of Mrs. Day's students is Tayla. Tayla's family recently moved to the United States from Saudi Arabia.

THE TEACHER: I love working with the kindergarten class. They are so full of energy and enthusiasm. I was very excited to welcome Tayla into my classroom a few weeks ago. There is now an even number of boys and girls in the classroom. I don't know much about Tayla's background. The only difference I see is that Tayla's mom wears Hijab, meaning that she covers her entire body and head except for her face and hands. Tayla has told the class that she will wear Hijab too when she turns nine years old. I have not felt comfortable speaking to the family about their background. The whole family speaks English, so how different could they be? The holiday play is a big deal to the center. A lot of time and effort are put into making sure everything is just right. After giving it a lot of thought, I have decided that all of the girls in the class should wear white leotards, red lipstick, and a crown decorated with five golden, glittery rings.

Is it ever appropriate to have a holiday program that focuses just on one religion or celebration? _____

_____

_____

Whose responsibility should it be to initiate a discussion about cultural needs? Mrs. Day? Tayla's family? _____

_____

_____

What are the potential problems with the costume Mrs. Day has selected? _____

_____

_____

THE CHILD: I am excited about my new school and new home, but I miss all of my friends back in Saudi Arabia and I especially miss my grandparents. Mom promised me that when we moved, I would be able to decorate my new bedroom any way I want. I hope Mom lets me paint the walls purple—it is my favorite color! I am also very excited about my new class. My new friend is Todd. His family lives down the street and sometimes we carpool to and from school. I think that Mrs. Day is very nice. She always wears very sparkly makeup on her eyes and bright red polish on her nails. I wish I could wear nail polish too, but my mom said "No way!" Today Mrs. Day told all of the students that she was putting a very special piece of paper in our mailboxes. She told everyone to make sure their parents read this letter so we would all have the right costume for the Christmas program. I am not sure what Christmas is all about, but the other children in the class are very excited, so I am looking forward to it too. My teacher told me, "You are really going to like Christmas in America." When I got home, my mom read the note from Mrs. Day and immediately looked upset. I was afraid that I had done something wrong; maybe the note was about the time I took a purple crayon from Todd. My mom tore the letter in half and threw it in the garbage.

What do you think about Mrs. Day's comment about Tayla enjoying Christmas in America? _____

_____

_____

Other than sending a note home, how else could the teacher have approached the families about her plans for the play? _____

_____

_____

What, if anything, should Mrs. Day explain to Tayla about the concept of Christmas?

_____

_____

_____

THE MOTHER: It has been quite an adventure since our family moved to the United States. The thought of leaving our family and home behind was terrifying, but we did it! We had hoped to purchase a home in a multicultural community. It is important to my husband and I that our children grow up in a place where they are accepted by our neighbors. I want my children to be able to become part of the American culture while holding onto our Islamic values. The school where I enrolled Tayla has several Hispanic and Chinese families but no others who shared our Muslim traditions. I sometimes receive strange looks when I wear my head scarf, but this is a part of my belief, just as it is my tradition not to wear makeup or revealing clothing out in public. I like the school's focus on academics, and they claimed to have an inclusive, multicultural learning environment. The children make frequent trips to a retirement home, and there is a strong focus on helping others within the community. That is an extremely important value for our family, and I was pleased to hear that it is reinforced at school. Since Tayla has started school, she has been talking about an upcoming play. I am unsure exactly what the program entails, but I assume it will encompass a variety of holiday celebrations.

How do you think Tayla's mother perceived the letter Mrs. Day had written about the

holiday program? _____

_____

_____

Should Tayla's mother have taken it upon herself to explain to Mrs. Day the family's

beliefs, including those surrounding modesty, prior to this incident? _____

_____

_____

How could this situation be resolved in a way that meets the needs of all involved?

_____

_____

_____

Communication Progress Report

Skill or Task	Range of Abilities		
	ALMOST ALWAYS	EMERGING SKILL	WILL LEARN
Staff members are sensitive to the needs of families.	☐	☐	☐
Staff members are able to initiate difficult conversations with families.	☐	☐	☐
Staff members are attentive and respectful in their communications with others.	☐	☐	☐
Families feel comfortable revealing relevant personal information to staff members.	☐	☐	☐
Staff members are willing to work as a team to accomplish projects and meet goals.	☐	☐	☐
The director is sensitive to the needs of all of the staff members.	☐	☐	☐
Staff members use good judgment in timing the initiation of discussions.	☐	☐	☐
All staff members are able to put the best interests of the children above their personal biases.	☐	☐	☐
Families are always notified in a timely and sensitive manner if concerning issues arise.	☐	☐	☐
Staff members maintain strict confidentiality with regard to family issues.	☐	☐	☐

The Ultimate Reference: Creation of a Family Handbook

COMING ATTRACTIONS

- How to apply the five W's to handbook design (who, why, where, when, and what)

- How to identify the information to be addressed in the handbook

- How to design your handbook so that it withstands the test of time

One of the easiest questions to address is the issue of *who* needs a handbook. The unequivocal answer is—you do! Your handbook serves as a "user's manual" for your child care center by providing a quick place for families to look up specific procedures and policies. Your handbook also serves as a great introduction to your center for new staff members or families considering enrollment in your program. While the time investment on your part to create a well-designed handbook can be considerable, your efforts will be rewarded many times over.

With so many competing demands on your time, you need to have a solid reason as to *why* developing a handbook is crucial to the success of your center. Your handbook will be the most important vehicle of communication. It can be used by all five of your target audiences and is an especially effective tool in communication with your primary audience, the current students and families. Well-informed families are usually satisfied customers.

Your families should be able to use your handbook to quickly and efficiently find the answers to a variety of routine questions. At pickup time, many families are rushed and distracted. In the excitement of showing off the day's art project and packing up a backpack, an important question may be forgotten. You want your families to have a place to turn to once they have left your center.

Once you have committed to writing a terrific handbook, *where* do you go from here? The most important step in the development of a great handbook is to allow yourself ample time. You can expect the process to evolve and grow in many different directions. If this is your first endeavor, start simple. Start gathering materials such as teacher biographies and old newspaper clippings about your center. Begin to make folders of information that you feel would be important to you, your staff, and your families.

Before you start writing, you need to establish a clear idea of the image of your center that you want to present. To do this, begin to think about what is important to you as a child care professional. For example, if you come from a medical

EFFECTIVE COMMUNICATION IN ACTION

FAMILY MEMBER: "My child's birthday is tomorrow and I forgot to ask his teacher if I could bring in cupcakes for the class. It is too late to call the center now. My child will be disappointed if he helps me make the cupcakes tonight and we can't bring them into the classroom tomorrow. He will also be disappointed if he is the only child in the class not to have a special celebration on his birthday. Maybe this is addressed in the handbook."

OUTCOME: After consulting the handbook, the family found that special snacks are permitted for birthdays, as long as enough is brought to share with the entire class. The handbook also recommended that cupcakes not be served as birthday treats because of low nutritional value. The family and child spent the evening preparing Fruit Popsicle treats to bring to school for the celebration.

background, an emphasis on nutrition may be important to you, and this should be reflected in the handbook. If you have children of your own, then the hours of operation and days the school will be closed will be a top priority to you. Obviously, all of these topics and many more will be included in your handbook. However, you need to remember that you will have a limited amount of space to present important aspects of your center to your families. The information you provide should be informative and concise. You want your handbook to read like a helpful reference manual rather than a meandering novel.

Take a look back at the answers to your questions for Activity 1.2. These questions were used to help you focus on your core message. This is the message that you want to have shine through in your handbook. Another way to develop the defining message of your handbook is to examine your everyday actions.

ACTIVITY 5.1 Putting Your Best Foot Forward

The answers to the following questions should help reveal to you the aspects of your center that you are most proud of. These are things that must be included in your handbook.

Imagine that a prospective family has dropped by your child care center to discuss enrolling their child.

What are the first materials you would present to the family? Why? _____

_____

_____

On a tour, what area of your center would you take them to first? Why? _____

_____

_____

Which staff member would you introduce them to first? Why? _____

_____

_____

The handbook should represent both who you are and what your center is about. You need to think about the type of atmosphere you would like to project. You can be creative, but you want to ensure that your style is always professional. Consider how

WHEN COMMUNICATION BREAKS DOWN

FAMILY: "I had no idea your center was closed the day after Thanksgiving. I arrived with my child on Friday morning to find a dark center and locked door. I needed to be at work by 9:00 A.M. and had not planned on trying to find a babysitter at the last minute. If I had known that you were going to be closed, I would have had much more time to prepare."

STAFF: "We sent out a message in every child's mailbox to notify families that the center would be closed. Perhaps the letter never made it home?"

COMMUNICATION LESSON: You cannot rely solely on letters placed in a child's mailbox to communicate important center information. There are too many variables that can result in the message being lost. Every family needs a handbook to serve as a consistent and reliable source of important information, such as details of holidays and closings. Additional informational opportunities such as bulletin boards and newsletters will be discussed in further detail in Chapters 6 and 7.

you can make your handbook unique, such as by including a child's drawings. Favorite phrases or photographs can break up the text and make your handbook more visually appealing. However, you should keep in mind that a consistent, professional tone in all of your written communications is important if you want your center to be recognized and accepted by your community as a business with staying power.

Your handbook should also provide the reader with an overall representation of the whole working staff. The handbook should reflect that you are proud of the people working at your center. Your staff should be represented as nurturing and loving individuals who take pride in the responsibility of caring for children.

At this point, you probably have lots of great ideas beginning to form, but *when* is the best time to put these ideas down on paper? Well, you can never start too early. Writing a handbook is a useful experience even if your center has not yet opened the doors for business. Putting together a handbook will give you the opportunity to develop your operational blueprint. From your previous experience in the field and discussion with other child care providers, you should be able to identify likely questions before they are even asked.

If your center is already open for business, the "timing" is even more immediate. Your audiences need to have all of the information you have been providing them verbally and through handouts, condensed into one professional packet. Almost every major commitment a person makes comes with a reference manual or contract; your families should expect the same level of commitment from your child care center.

The most important part of the handbook is *what* you include. For most handbooks, the information you want to communicate to your families can be divided into four different areas: Introduction, Policies and Procedures, Curriculum, and Extras.

Start with a blank sheet of paper for each category and start listing either materials that you have available or that need to be developed. This would be a good time to go through folders that you have already started to make for yourself containing materials that you thought were important to your center. You may also want to make a "To Do List" of materials and writings that you think you may want to include in your handbook.

Remember your handbook should be uncomplicated and easy to read. Save all of your "educational terminology" for another time. Use simple terms that will be understood by a wide range of adults. Remember that what may sound simple for you or your teachers to understand may sound foreign to families.

Let's spend some time going into each one of the four sections in some more detail.

Introduction

First impressions are often lasting, so make sure yours is a good one. Although the introduction is not the heart of your handbook, it should motivate the reader to continue. A handbook that is packed with information will not do any good if it remains unread.

On your first page you need to welcome the reader to both your center and the handbook. Include one strength of your center, something that distinguishes you from the competition. This is especially important if you plan to use your handbook as a promotional tool for prospective families. Let families know in the welcome section that although this handbook will serve as an excellent resource for the center, they are also encouraged to ask questions and to visit the center often. While the handbook is an important tool for communication, it cannot and should not replace face-to-face interaction between families and staff.

The introduction is also the perfect place to explain your philosophy on child care. Let your families know what is important to you and your staff. You also need to give the reader some concrete examples of how you support your philosophy. If your philosophy is that children learn best when they are having fun, you will want to make reference to the numerous educational toys in your center and the curriculum, which allows children to choose from a multitude of tasks designed to teach each skill.

ACTIVITY 5.2 Customize the Welcome Section

Use the template provided on page 76 to design a welcome section to fit the needs of your center.

Welcome Section Template

Print this form from the enclosed CD!

> **Welcome**
>
> Welcome to [Center]! We are pleased that you have trusted us with your child's early education. Our primary goal is [enter Center goal here].
>
> Designed for discriminating families, [Center] is the premier learning center in [enter town]. Since [enter year established] we have offered [enter programs available]. Individual attention to each child's needs is commonplace. Just as important, the center has developed a comprehensive and engaging curriculum for each of our programs.
>
> This handbook will inform you about our high-quality programs, general policies, and procedures to make your experience with [Center] an enjoyable one. [Center] staff and management are committed to meeting the needs of each child and family.
>
> After review of this handbook, we encourage you to ask questions and refer to this book often. Families are always welcome at [Center] and appointments are never necessary. Please feel free to stop by the center at any time. We look forward to serving your family and promise to provide a warm and loving environment for your child while promoting individual development to the fullest.

It is important to provide your families with some background information about your child care center. In the history section, you should provide the reader with the story about how your center has developed into what it is today. If your center is relatively new, you can describe how your interest in child care began and what steps you have taken in your career that have led you to this point. If your center has undergone any name or facility changes over the years, you should include that information here. A stable environment is very important to most families; you should end this section by reaffirming your commitment to continued growth and development. Your families will need to know that your center is here to stay.

Next, you want to focus on the people who make your center a great place to be, the teaching staff. This section should not introduce specific staff members, as this will require your handbook to be updated frequently, but you should introduce the professional staff as a whole. If you only employ college-educated teachers, be sure this is stated in the handbook. You will also want to make reference to the ways your staff continues to learn and grow. Opportunities for continuing education classes, professional development courses, or special training should also be addressed in this section.

ACTIVITY 5.3 Customize the Philosophy Section

Use the template provided on page 77 to design a philosophy section to fit the needs of your center.

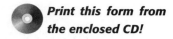
Print this form from the enclosed CD!

Philosophy Section Template

Philosophy

[Center] was founded on the philosophy that [enter center philosophy here].

Our care is based on a nurturing attitude that is expressed through:

- respecting each child and his or her abilities.
- fostering intellectual, social, physical, and emotional development.
- developing positive attitudes through positive experiences.

To support our philosophy, we:

- employ and train skilled professional staff with special qualities needed to work with young children.
- develop program goals for each age group and provide children with support to reach these goals.
- maintain bright, inviting, cheerful facilities with ample space for small, well-supervised groups.
- [Additional activities to support philosophy and center goal].

[Center] curricula are drawn from the latest educational concepts and teaching techniques. We take the very best from different schools of thought and apply our knowledge to develop a curriculum that promotes learning for all children.

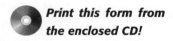
Print this form from the enclosed CD!

Teaching Staff Section Template

Teaching Staff

We take great pride in our professional staff, their qualifications, their credentials, and their ability to work together to maintain a safe, nurturing, and productive environment for your child.

[Center] proudly employs a college-educated teaching staff. Their degrees are in education and other child-related areas of learning. In addition, each teacher receives special training from [Center] prior to working with the children. [Center] teachers also attend numerous continuing education classes every year. Teachers are assigned to specific age groups based on their interest and experience to ensure the highest quality instruction and care for your child.

ACTIVITY 5.4 Customize the Teaching Staff Section

Use the template provided above to design a teaching staff section to fit the needs of your center.

ACTIVITY 5.5 Determining Your Goals and Objectives

The list provided on page 79 encompasses a wide variety of goals and objectives. You can use this list as a starting point for determining the goals and objectives that best suit your center. You should rate each point according to how applicable you feel it is to your center, curricula, and philosophy. You should ask families and staff members to do the same. You can use this information to put together a list of goals and objectives that are unique to your center.

The introductory section should conclude with a list of your center's goals and objectives. You should let families know what they can expect their children to learn while they are in your care. Be sure that the goals and objectives you include are inclusive enough to be applicable to a variety of age groups.

Your introduction should provide your families with a solid background of who you are and what you believe in. Let your families know they made the right decision in entrusting their child to you.

Policies and Procedures

Policies and procedures seem to have a life of their own. You only need to be in business for a short time to realize how crucial this infrastructure will be to your business. You need to explain exactly what families can expect of you and what you expect of them. When you are developing your handbook, try to anticipate potential problems before they arise. One of the most important sections of your policies and procedures is your Emergency Plans and Procedures section. Families need to feel secure that if an emergency did arise, your center has established plans to ensure the continued safety of their children.

Policies and Procedures may be the most utilized section of your handbook. A complete Policies and Procedures section should answer many of the most common questions families have. Your handbook will serve as a written reminder to families of what they can expect of you, and in return, what you expect of them.

Arrivals and departures. The day begins with the arrival of the children, and this is where your Policies and Procedures section should begin. Arrival and departure should be an easy transition; families do not want to leave their children in a chaotic environment. Help ease children and families into the day by having a well-defined procedure.

Here are some areas that need to be covered in the Arrivals and Departures section:

- What are your hours of operation? Clearly state the opening and closing time for your center.
- Explain the need for prompt arrival and pickup; experience has shown that children are more at ease when they arrive and depart on time.

Goals and Objectives Template

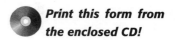

Goal or Objective of the Center	Importance Ranking				
	Very Important	Important	Neutral	Less Important	Not Important
To care for all children in a warm, protective, and affectionate environment					
To reinforce each child's cultural heritage through song, literature, poetry, and crafts on appropriate holidays and anniversaries					
To demonstrate that each child is a special person					
To meet the physical needs of each child					
To instill in each child a feeling of autonomy and self-respect					
To establish respect for others and their possessions					
To develop gross and fine motor skills through indoor and outdoor play					
To provide opportunities for learning and social interaction through stimulating daily activities					
To introduce art, science, social studies, math concepts, reading readiness, dramatic play, manipulative activities, language, music, and movement					
To monitor each child's development and provide regular progress reports to parents					
To allow all children to appreciate people, customs, and cuisines from other cultures					
To develop in each child an appreciation for beauty and nature					
To encourage parent involvement					
To promote intellectual and emotional growth					
To encourage open and honest communication					
To create a feeling of independence and confidence in the child through a mastery of life skills					
Teachers are nurturing adults, who have children's best interest at heart.					
The staff is able to adjust the daily program to meet children's special needs and interests.					

- Does your center reserve the right to discontinue service to any family due to chronic early arrivals and late pickup? If so, state this.
- Detail any security measures (sign-in books, security codes, name tags, etc.) you have put into place to keep the children safe while they are in your care. Explain how this will affect the arrival and departure procedures.
- Who is responsible for removing the child's outerwear and settling them with their class? If this is a parent responsibility, be sure this is clearly stated.
- Are children permitted to bring breakfast from home to eat at the center?
- Where do food and extra clothing belong? Is any special labeling required?
- Stress the importance of quick departures. Some families may not realize that your teachers have another class to prepare for.
- Clearly communicate what the penalty will be for a late pickup (e.g., $10.00 for every 15 minutes or fraction thereof that a child is left past the end of program hours).
- What kind of notification is required for someone other than a parent to pick up a child from the program? Will a phone call suffice or is written permission needed? Will the person picking up the child need to bring proper identification into the center?
- What is expected of families who will be bringing siblings into the center for arrival or departure time? Are siblings allowed to play on center equipment? Are teachers responsible for monitoring sibling behavior?
- Can children enter the center on their own or must they be accompanied?
- Are there any special parking considerations that need to be addressed?
- What is the plan for a forgotten child? How many staff members will stay to accompany a forgotten child? How will the center attempt to contact the family or other emergency contacts? At what point will the child be turned over to the local authorities?

Enrollment. Enrollment in a child care center can involve a lot more paperwork than many families expect. This section of the handbook should address what will be expected of families prior to their child's first day. Don't let missing paperwork spoil the experience of a child's first day. Help families adequately prepare by providing them with a list of items they will be expected to complete prior to the first day of school.

The following items should be discussed in the Enrollment section of your handbook:

- Which forms are required to be completed prior to the first day of school?
  —fully completed registration form
  —physician's report showing that the child is current on all immunizations and has had a physical exam within the last 12 months; this must be signed by the physician

—signed consent forms

—nonrefundable registration fee for the first year (you may also want to include the registration fee for subsequent years if different)

- Will families be given notice that a physical exam form is about to expire?

- How should families let the center know if contact information has changed?

- Is there a trial period for all children? If so, how long is it and what happens at the end of the trial period?

- Does the center retain the right to discontinue its service to any family at the center's discretion, due to issues including payment problems, family problems, child behavior problems, late or early arrivals or pickups, bringing sick children to school, and so on?

Discipline procedures. Discipline procedures can vary greatly from family to family. Before enrolling their child in your center, families need to understand and agree with your disciplinary policy. You should provide clear examples of the types of discipline that may be administered to a child in the program. You should also state what types of discipline will not be employed at the center. Remember that what you put into writing needs to be followed in the same way every time by every member of your staff.

Emergency plans and procedures. The section of your handbook that covers emergency plans and procedures should be one of the areas you devote the most time to. You need to have plans that are not only well thought out but also practical, given the physical environment of your center. Before committing a fire emergency procedure to paper, you may want to practice it at your center. Sometimes the most concrete plans go awry when put into action. Your emergency plans and procedures need to be read, discussed, and understood by both families and staff members. When an emergency occurs, you want the correct procedure to be an automatic reaction; the heat of the moment is not the time for questions to arise. You will need emergency plans for at least three scenarios: a fire emergency, minor injury to a child, and serious injury to a child. Depending on the location of your center, you may also need to develop plans for natural disasters such as tornadoes or earthquakes. Let's review the three major emergency types in more detail.

ACTIVITY 5.6 Customize the Discipline Procedures Section

Use the template provided on page 82 to design a Discipline section to fit the needs of your center.

Print this form from the enclosed CD!

Discipline Procedures Section Template

Discipline Procedures

[Center] discipline policy adheres to the guidelines presented in Jennifer Birckmayer's "Seven Procedures of Discipline" (*Discipline Is Not a Dirty Word*. New York: Cornell Cooperative Extension, 1995).

1. Tell children what they can do instead of what they can't.
2. Protect and preserve children's feelings that they are lovable and capable.
3. Offer children choices only when they are willing to abide by their decisions.
4. Change the environment instead of the child's behavior.
5. Work with children instead of against them.
6. Give children safe limits they can understand. Recognize their feelings without accepting their actions. Maintain your authority calmly and consistently. If children break rules, allow them to experience the consequences of their behavior.
7. Set a good example. Speak and act only in ways you want children to speak and act.

These guidelines provide a framework for ensuring effective disciplinary situations with the children. Although each disciplinary situation is unique, an example of accepted methods would include:

1. Tell the child we do not like what he or she is doing and why.
2. Take the toy (for example) from the child.
3. Redirect the child to a different toy or activity.
4. Remove the child from the group (but within eyesight of the teacher) until the child is ready to rejoin the group and follow the rules.
5. When a child is removed from the group, he or she is to be isolated for one minute for each year of age. After that time, the teacher will confer with the child and suggest he or she return to the group.
6. Our policy is designed to teach children how to:
   A. use words
   B. walk away
   C. ask for help

The center does not, and will not, employ any of the following disciplinary procedures:

1. harsh or abusive tone of voice with the children
2. physical punishment, including spanking, hitting, shaking, or grabbing
3. any punishment that would humiliate, frighten, or subject a child to neglect

Physical restraint will not be used unless it is necessary to protect the safety and health of the child or others.

Fire alarms. The squeal of a fire alarm is a frightening noise for both adults and children. Your center should have in place a fire emergency plan that is practiced on a regular basis. In the event of a real fire, both the children and staff members will be prepared. In this situation, careful preparation truly can make the difference between life and death. Your Fire Emergency Policy should address the following:

- How often are fire drills practiced at the center?
- Will families be given advance notice of a fire drill?
- How are children taught to react to a fire drill? Most centers have a six-step system like the one listed next.
- Which staff member will be responsible for checking the bathrooms and all other areas to ensure that all children are safely outside?
- If the fire has not yet set off the alarm, who will be responsible for notifying the fire department?
- Has an emergency pickup area been established at a local fire department or police station?
- If the staff were unable to retrieve emergency contact members before leaving the building, will one staff member remain on-site for direction of families to an emergency pickup area?

Fire drill system.

1. Listen to the teacher for instructions.
2. Line up immediately at the door and remain quiet.
3. Stop what you are doing and follow the teacher outside, without coats, toys, or umbrellas.
4. Leave the building through the closest exit (exits should always be clearly marked).
5. Move as far away from the building as possible, following the teacher to the safe meeting spot.
6. The teacher will take attendance to ensure all children are accounted for.

Child injuries. When working with children, occasional injuries are inevitable. Your handbook should describe to families how injuries, both minor and serious, are treated at your center. From a scraped knee to a broken arm or worse, you need to reassure families that your center and staff are equipped to respond to their child's needs.

ACTIVITY 5.7 Customize the Injury Treatment Section

Use the template provided on page 84 to design an injury treatment section to fit the needs of your center.

Injury Treatment Section Template

Print this form from the enclosed CD!

Procedure for Minor Injury to a Child

- A staff person certified in first aid by the American Red Cross will be present at all times.
- First aid treatment (i.e., washing skin surface, small bandages, etc.) will be administered by the child's teacher or school nurse.
- A written Emergency Treatment Form will be completed by the child's teacher or school nurse and signed by the teacher in charge. This form will go home with the child and will provide specifics about the injury sustained and treatment administered.
- Depending on the severity of the injury, the child's family will be called immediately to take him or her to a physician.
- The child's teacher or school nurse will remain with the child and continue to apply first aid as needed.

Procedure for Serious Injury to a Child

- Certified first aid personnel, the school nurse, and/or the teacher will remain with the child and appropriately apply first aid.
- A second staff person or director will call the ambulance, retrieve the child's file, and call the family and authorized emergency contact.
- The child's teacher and/or person in charge will ride with the child in the ambulance to the hospital. The child's file goes along in the ambulance to the hospital.
- A parent or authorized emergency contact person meets the teacher at the hospital to authorize treatment for the child. Signed consent for treatment is in the child's file if a parent or contact cannot be reached.

Inclement weather. Although you do your best to give families plenty of advance warning about days when your center will be closed, it is likely that inclement weather may force you to make quick decisions. Your handbook should contain a section that discusses how families will be notified of a closing due to severe weather. Your Inclement Weather Policy should include the following:

- How will families be notified of a closing due to severe weather? Will this information be broadcast via radio or television?
- Will your center follow the public school closing schedule?
- How will families be notified if a decision is made to close once the school day is in progress?
- If the center is unable to contact a child's family and it is deemed necessary to remove the child from the center, how will the child be transported to the emergency center?
- How will families be notified if children have been removed from the center?
- Will the same procedures be followed in the case of civil defense emergencies?

Family visits. Your families will be relying on your staff to provide them with feedback on their child's intellectual and social development. Your plan for keeping families informed should be described in the Family Visit section of the handbook. Families should know how often they can expect family-teacher conferences and what other methods will be used to keep them informed about daily activities at the center. Newsletters, child mailboxes, bulletin boards, and weekly schedules are all useful communication tools.

Sick children. Many families may have questions related to when it is appropriate to bring a child who is not feeling well to school. It is important for the health and well-being of all the children at the center that children who have an illness that may be contagious remain at home until they have recovered. The definition of a "sick child" may be variable depending on the family, so it is important to include in your Sick Child Procedures section symptoms that indicate that a child should remain at home. It is also important to put a plan into place to safely accommodate the over-the-counter or prescription medications a recovering child may need to bring to school.

Nutrition. Growing children need to eat nutritious foods on a regular basis in order to reach their full potential. Depending on the length of your daily program, you may find it necessary to supply the children with snacks at designated intervals during the day. Your center may also be equipped to provide full meals in place of family-provided lunches. Your handbook should describe how snacks, lunches, and birthdays are handled at your center. You can also use this section to reference the USDA Food Pyramid Guidelines for children and provide an example of what a lunch falling within these guidelines will look like.

Tuition. In order to maintain the high standards and quality of your center, you need to have a tuition schedule that your families are willing to adhere to. Child care tuition can be a substantial investment for families, and you should respect this by giving plenty of notice before a tuition increase or payment schedule change. Some issues that need to be addressed in the Tuition Schedule section of the handbook are as follows:

- Families should be aware of the day when tuition is expected and the penalties for late payments.
- What is the center's policy in regard to credit for missed days due to illness or vacation?
- What are acceptable methods of payment?
- Who should the family speak to if they have a question or concern regarding their bill for tuition?

ACTIVITY 5.8 Customize the Sick Child Procedures Section

Use the template provided on page 86 to design a Sick Child Procedures section to fit the needs of your center.

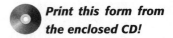
Print this form from the enclosed CD!

Sick Child Procedure Section Template

Sick Child Procedures

For the health and safety of all the children, it is mandatory that sick children not be brought to school. If your child has any of the following symptoms during the night, he or she will not be admitted the following morning for the safety of the other children.

- fever greater than 100 degrees F
- vomiting
- diarrhea
- pink eyes with drainage
- cough with congestion and excessive nasal discharge

The center's established policy for an ill child's return:

- Fever free for 24 hours
- Chicken pox: one week after onset (or when lesions are crusted)
- Strep: 24 hours after initial medication
- Vomiting/Diarrhea: 24 hours after last episode
- Conjunctivitis: 24 hours after initial medication or when without drainage

Children who need to continue medication for an illness after they are able to safely return to school will be given their medication provided that:

- An authorized medication form is completed by the child's physician and signed by the parent or guardian
- The medication is in the original container with the prescription label intact
- Over-the-counter medication must have a form signed by the family and the child's physician in order for the center to administer the medication

Medications are administered by the nurse or by authorized staff members who have completed a medication administration class.

Curriculum

Today's society wants to see their children learn. Families are comforted knowing that more is going on in their child's day than just playing. By including a curriculum in your handbook, you can illustrate that a child's school day involves both learning and having fun while at school. This will not only put your families at ease, but it will also let your teachers know what is expected of them.

Your curriculum is integral to the everyday functioning of your center. Just as you would not set off on a cross-country adventure without a map, no center can expect children to effectively learn without a well-developed curriculum. Your curriculum should be designed to specifically meet the educational and developmental needs of each age group you care for. Since the needs of preschoolers differ significantly from the needs of elementary schoolchildren, you should consider developing separate sections for each age group in your center.

Each age group curriculum section should include information on the typical level of social and emotional development displayed by the specific age group, curriculum objectives, areas of instruction, and sample daily schedule. Communicating the curriculum to your families is discussed in detail in Chapter 6.

Extras

What does your center offer that distinguishes it from others in the area? These "extras" should be proudly displayed in your handbook. Extracurricular programs such as gymnastics, tutoring, art, or dance should be described in this section. It is also important to include information regarding the tuition and registration needs for these programs.

Does your center offer a summer camp? If so, be sure to include information about the field trips, programs, and exciting opportunities that allow the children to make the most of the summer camp experience. Many families see the summer months as a time to relax and have fun, and your curriculum should be adjusted accordingly.

Does your center organize any activities to help make your community a better place for all? If so, be sure to include the details of the programs you are involved in or associated with.

Finally, here is a word on getting the most use out of your handbook. The handbook should be developed with an eye on the future. The information should "pass the test of time." You have likely invested a great deal of time and money in preparing and printing your handbook, so you should make the most of your investment by ensuring that it can be used for years to come. Avoid making any specific references to staff members or programs, as these may change on a frequent basis. You also should avoid putting dates into your handbook, or you will be forced to update it on an annual basis. Be sure that all of your policies and procedures are well thought out before you commit them to writing. Once your families have in writing what they can expect, it will be very difficult to alter the policy. Have your staff read over your handbook and provide feedback and suggestions. You need them to believe in the material presented in the handbook so you can present a unified image to your families. You may also want to consider asking a few families to read the handbook before it is finalized. Ask them if it meets their needs. After all, this is the audience you designed the handbook for.

Communication Progress Report

Handbook Section	Range of Abilities		
	ALWAYS MEET	**EMERGING SKILL**	**WILL IMPROVE**
Introduction welcomes the reader to learn more about the center.	☐	☐	☐
Your philosophy is clearly stated and reflects what is most important to you and your staff.	☐	☐	☐
The talents of your staff are showcased in the Teaching Staff section.	☐	☐	☐
The goals and objectives of your center reflect the unique environment it provides.	☐	☐	☐
Policies and procedures are explained for everyday occurrences, such as arrival, lunch, and discipline.	☐	☐	☐
Plans for emergency situations are well thought out and complete.	☐	☐	☐
The staff has been adequately trained on all procedures and policies, including those important in emergency situations.	☐	☐	☐
Good overviews have been provided for each age-specific curriculum.	☐	☐	☐
A sample daily schedule has been included, so families are able to identify the likely activities their children are participating in during any part of the day.	☐	☐	☐
The extras the center offers have been explained.	☐	☐	☐
The handbook has been designed to exclude references to specific items that change frequently.	☐	☐	☐
The handbook has been reviewed and critiqued by both staff and families prior to printing to ensure their needs have been met.	☐	☐	☐

Using Handouts and Newsletters to Keep Your Audiences Informed

COMING ATTRACTIONS

- How to determine the type of information that is most effectively communicated through handouts or newsletters

- How to provide the materials to staff and families in a comprehensive welcome packet

- How to structure your materials so they are informative without being overwhelming

COMMUNICATION

Although your handbook will contain information that is integral to the functioning of your center, it alone is not sufficient to communicate all of your policies and center happenings. In order to keep your families adequately informed, you will need to use a variety of handouts and newsletters. Although both handouts and newsletters are forms of written communication, they differ in their content and purpose. The table below provides clarification on the differences between the two types of documents.

Differences between Handouts and Newsletters

	Handout	**Newsletter**
Communication Purpose	Important information on policies and procedures	Information on what has happened at school and future happenings
Applicability	Usually applicable to all families within the center	Usually applicable to only specific groups or programs
Need for Updates	Relatively long term; will require annual review but not necessarily revision	Relatively short term, will require weekly or monthly updates to stay current
Presentation of the Document	Professionally presented, formal letter or other structured format	Creative focus, can be handwritten
Inclusion in Handbook	May also be briefly addressed in handbook	Should not be included in handbook due to transient nature of information
Relationship to State-Mandated Regulations	May be information the state requires to be distributed and posted or information related to national accreditation	Never required by the state for distribution as a component of licensing, not required to be posted
Examples	One-Page Policy Statement, Peanut Policy, Child Abuse and Neglect Policy, Emergency Procedures, Confidential Staff Policies	Weekly Coming Attractions, Health Alerts, Tuition Reminders, Director's Newsletters

Handouts

It is important to note that there is not an absolute distinction between what constitutes a handout and what constitutes a newsletter. Information one center considers best as a handout may be considered by another to be more appropriate in a newsletter. As long as the information is being appropriately communicated to your audiences, there is no need to belabor the task of discrimination between the two types of written communication. We will first discuss a variety of handouts, including One-Page Policy Statement, Peanut Policy, Child Abuse and Neglect Policy, Emergency Procedures, and Confidential Staff Policies, before turning our attention to types of newsletters.

One-Page Policy Statement

Handouts can serve multiple purposes. They can inform your families about policies that were not covered in the handbook, review amendments to policies previously presented to families in the handbook or elsewhere, or serve as reminders of important current policies. The more informed your parents are about the procedures and policies of the center, the less likely you are to run into conflict regarding these areas. However, the posting and distribution of specific policy statements is more than good business, it is also the law. Every state in the nation has set forth specific rules and regulations that must be followed in order for a center to be licensed. Portions of the state regulations discuss the center policies and the disclosure of these policies to your families. While each state is unique, it is fairly standard to require that a licensed center maintain general operating policies. These policies must be in written format and reviewed annually. In general, centers are required to have operating policies including, but not limited to:

- admission, which includes a health record and ages of children enrolled
- agreements with parents
- parent involvement
- medication policies if applicable
- content and times of meals and snacks
- provisional enrollment period
- days and hours of operation, including sick days, holidays, and vacations
- withdrawal of children
- access to program and facility

Some of these policies have been addressed in the handbook, but to include them all would make the handbook a long, cumbersome read. Instead, families can be informed of these policies through a one-page policy statement handout. The handout would include all of the policies required by the state as well as any additional standard policy of operation at your center. The one-page handout is not the appropriate place for lengthy policies such as the Child Abuse and Neglect Policy or the Emergency Procedure Plan. Policies that require in-depth consideration will be presented in individual handouts.

ACTIVITY 6.1 Creating a One-Page Policy Statement

Using the template provided on page 92, create a one-page policy statement that includes all of the required general operating policies. Some of the policies found on the one-page policy statement may also be discussed in the handbook.

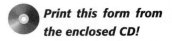

Print this form from the enclosed CD!

[Center] Policy Statement

Please take a moment to familiarize yourself with the [Center's] Policy Statement. Regulations have been adopted to meet specific requirements to maintain state licensing and to provide families with the highest quality child care. We encourage you to ask questions about any provision if you are unsure of its intent.

1. Hours of operation are 7:00 A.M. to 6:00 P.M., Monday through Friday. We will accept enrolled children any time after 7:00 A.M.

2. A current completed health form (yearly visits) must be on file for each child at all times. The state health department requires that each certificate be signed by a doctor and show that the child has been immunized against polio, diphtheria, pertussis, tetanus, measles, mumps, and rubella.

3. In the event of severe weather, please call the center or listen to (provide station) on your radio prior to bringing your child to the center.

4. A child who has a fever, vomiting, or diarrhea during the night will not be admitted the following morning for the safety of the other children. If a child becomes ill during the day, we will notify the parent to have the child picked up as quickly as possible. Only people with names listed on the emergency sheet will be allowed to pick up the child. If a child does not attend due to illness, payment is still expected.

5. If a child is in need of any medication during the school-day, a Medication Permission Form must be signed by the child's doctor and parent. Forms are available on the table in the lobby.

6. All payments should be made out to the center. Payment for all programs is due on the first day of the week (or month).

7. Licensing and scheduling restrictions prevent credit for holiday, sick, and inclement weather days for full-day preschool and after-school care. Full-day preschool and after-school care children are allowed up to two weeks' absence for vacation during the year from September through June where payments are not required. The children must be absent a full week for this to apply. *Children attending the center after-school care program, who attend the center full-time during December and Spring school vacations or attend full-time for any portion of the vacation weeks, will be charged the full-time child care weekly rate.*

8. Half-day preschool tuition is based on the total amount of days in the calendar year from September through June. Tuition is a yearly fee divided into ten monthly payments.

9. A non-refundable $75.00 registration fee covering supplies, books, and liability insurance is required for all children their first year of attendance. Thereafter, the fee is $50.00.

10. All lunch boxes are required to have a freezer pack in them, regardless of the content, in accordance with state regulations. The center provides milk during lunch and a morning and afternoon snack. If the child requires special food, the parent is required to provide that food. Occasionally special snacks for birthdays and activities will be provided. Please be sure to let us know of any food allergies or special dietary considerations.

11. The center retains the right to discontinue its service to any family at the center's discretion. This includes, but is not limited to, payment problems, parental problems, child behavior problems, and bringing in sick children.

12. Parents are welcome to visit at any time during operating hours.

13. Children's articles/food should be labeled. We are not responsible for lost or broken items.

14. At no time will any child be subjected to physical or demeaning verbal punishment. Discipline will be in the form of discussing the problem with the child. If necessary, the child may be disciplined by temporary separation from the other children, and activities. However, the child will never be away from the care of a teacher or aide.

15. Late charges of $10.00 for every 15 minutes or part thereof will apply to any child left at the center past the 6:00 P.M. closing. Please call if you know you will be late. If the teacher has not been able to contact anyone to come and collect the child and the child remains at the center until 8:00 P.M., the child will then be considered an abandoned child and the police will be notified.

16. We ask parents to give at least two weeks' notice of their plans to withdraw their children.

17. If your child will not be attending school because of illness, vacation, or a special visitor, please give us a call. We look forward to seeing your child and appreciate notice if he or she will not be here.

18. Field trips that are educational and fun are planned during the year. Children in attendance are expected to participate. Due to staffing considerations, we cannot provide care for children who do not come on the trip.

19. Students must be potty trained by the start of school. We ask that students do not wear pull-ups. Underpants are much easier for students to manage themselves. We understand that sometimes little ones have bathroom accidents.

WHEN COMMUNICATION BREAKS DOWN

FAMILY: "My son was very excited to bring his new Barney stuffed animal to show the class during Show and Tell. He just told me that you made him leave the toy in his cubby all day. Why?"

STAFF: "I am sorry but several children in our center have contracted head lice and I could not permit any stuffed animals from home into the classroom."

FAMILY: "Are you insinuating that the lice came from my house? I resent this implication!"

OUTCOME: The family member stormed out of the classroom and refused to discuss the issue further. The teacher did not get a chance to clear up the confusion until the next day. The family and teacher were never able to reestablish a good communicative relationship.

COMMUNICATION LESSON: A change to center policy needs to be well communicated to all of your families. In this situation, the teacher should have allowed one more day of toys in the classroom and then ensured that all the parents had received the notice. This situation made a family feel responsible for a situation out of their control.

It is impossible to anticipate issues that will arise over the course of the year for inclusion into the handbook. If you are forced to amend center policy or add an additional policy you should inform your families through a handout. Your handout should always include the rationale for the change or addition. For example, your handbook may state that children are permitted to bring toys from home. However, during a head lice outbreak you may decide that it is in the best interest of the children to restrict toys brought in from home. Your policy handout should give specifics as to which policy is being amended and how long the amendment will be followed. Families that enroll in your center after the policy addition or amendment should be provided the handout that supercedes the information delineated in the handbook along with their copy of the handbook. Materials such as these should always be dated. Your center should strive to keep changes to the handbook to a minimum, as multiple changes can suggest lack of preparedness. Multiple changes to the handbook will also necessitate the need for a formal handbook revision.

Peanut Policy

An example of a policy that you may find necessary to enact after a handbook has been published is a peanut policy. Due to the increasing number of children who have serious allergic reactions to peanuts, many centers are proactively addressing the dangers by prohibiting peanut products at the center. If your handbook was developed and published more than two years ago, it is likely that a policy such as this one was never considered. Your center could address the issue through a handout, eliminating the need for a complete revision of the handbook.

ACTIVITY 6.2 Creating a Peanut Policy

Using the template provided below, create a peanut policy statement that includes the rationale for the new policy, delineation of whom this policy affects, information about how families can implement the policy, and the person who should be contacted if further clarification is needed.

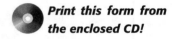

Print this form from the enclosed CD!

Peanut Policy Template

Peanut Policy

In recent years the center has been aware of an increase in the number of children with life-threatening allergies. The most common of these allergens is *peanuts*. In [year peanut policy implemented], [Center] adopted its *no-peanut policy*. This is the only way to prevent an allergic child from developing a reaction. Due to the nature of the allergy, isolation is not an effective option.

We are asking for your understanding and assistance in maintaining the health and safety of all children while in our care. Please *do not send* any peanut or nut-containing products. These include the obvious peanut butter and jelly sandwich, peanut butter cups, candies, cookies, and cereal bars. You should also be aware of other products that may contain peanuts according to their labels. These are *plain* M&M's, Mini Chips Ahoy cookies, and *low fat* Cheez Nips.

Some products that we have found to be nut free are:

Oreos	Skittles	Applesauce	Pudding
Twizzlers	Animal Crackers	Pretzels	Fig Newtons
Nilla Wafers	Potato Chips	Gummy treats	CheezIts

We hope you understand the seriousness of this problem and our efforts to prevent a medical emergency. We never want any child to experience a severe reaction, nor do we want any child to witness another having this reaction.

Thank you for your cooperation. Please feel free to stop by the office if you have any additional questions regarding this policy.

EFFECTIVE COMMUNICATION IN ACTION

FAMILY: "I brought peanut butter cups for Adam to share with his class on his birthday. He told me the teacher refused to let him share the treats at snack time. What is the problem?"

STAFF: "I am sorry this happened to Adam today. I know his birthday is a special day for celebrations. We have many children at the center who have life-threatening peanut allergies. It was decided last year that it was in the best interest of all the children to prohibit any peanut-containing items from our classroom. The school has established a no-peanut policy. This policy was placed in all of the mailboxes on the first day of school and we discussed it at Family Orientation Night. Here is a copy of our policy. I am sorry that you were not made aware of it earlier. I am sure we can still make Adam's birthday celebration a happy event. Can we celebrate his special day again tomorrow?"

OUTCOME: After the staff acknowledged Adam's hurt feelings and apologized for the misunderstanding, the family agreed to bring in another treat the next day for the birthday celebration.

In addition to informing your families about new policies not found in the handbook or changes to existing policies, handouts are also used as reminders of important current policies such as emergency procedures or child abuse and neglect reporting. When families receive a great deal of information at one time, as they are presented in the handbook, some of the included information may be overlooked. Distributions of handouts are a way to ensure that your families have read and have the opportunity to ask questions about your most important center policies.

Child Abuse and Neglect Policy

Some of the most important and most enforced policies are those relating to child abuse and neglect. Each state has a dedicated Web site covering these topics, and your handout concerning the topic should be developed using the materials provided by the state. The decision on whether the child abuse policy should be presented in the handbook, through a handout, or both is center directed. The caution against putting it in the handbook is that the policy is subject to change at any time, and the depth and breadth of the change are determined by the state, without center input. If you include the child abuse policy in your handbook, you will need to issue an update in the event of an important change to the policy. Most states also require every center to post the child abuse policy in a conspicuous location. This is easily facilitated if the policy is presented in handout form.

Your child abuse and neglect policy should include the following elements:

- definitions of child abuse and child neglect as put forth by your state
- a statement that all child care professionals are mandated reporters of child abuse and neglect
- the phone numbers for the state Child Abuse and Neglect Hotline
- statement that mandatory reporters can not be held liable, either civil or criminal, for reporting what they believe to be an instance of child abuse, unless the reporter is also the abuser
- penalties for knowingly making a false report
- signs and symptoms of child abuse
- what to do if you witness abuse or neglect by a center staff member
- what steps will be taken if a staff member is accused of abuse
- how to obtain medical treatment for a victim of abuse or neglect

To ensure that your child abuse policy is complete and accurate under state law, you should consider having it reviewed by a state official or lawyer knowledgeable in the subject area.

Emergency Procedures

The Emergency Procedure Plan is another document required by most states to be posted in a conspicuous area of the center. Many of these plans are also reviewed in your handbook but when the policy deals with a life or death situation, reinforcement is always a prudent idea. Your Emergency Procedure Plan should cover what should be done in the following situations (as discussed in more detail in Chapter 5):

- fire emergency
- emergency evacuation
- severe weather conditions
- minor injury to a child
- serious injury to a child

Also posted should be a comprehensive references list of emergency phone numbers. Included in this list should be 911 and additional numbers needed for the fire department, police department, ambulance company, bus company, nearest hospital, poison control, all local schools, alarm company, medical consultant, dental consultant, child abuse and neglect hotline, canine control, mental health services, radio stations for severe weather reporting, and building maintenance or repair. If you are ever part of an emergency situation, you do not want to waste valuable time trying to obtain the appropriate contact phone numbers. All emergency procedures and phone numbers should be posted in a location that can be quickly reached. This may mean posting multiple copies of the policy if your center occupies a large space.

Confidential Staff Policies

All of the previously discussed policies are applicable to both staff members and center families. There are a few policies that relate solely to the staff of the center, however. One is the procedure for attempted child abduction. A good center has to be prepared for a variety of emergencies, and with custody battles overflowing the courts, the possibility of child abduction cannot be overlooked. This policy should be presented to the staff of the center but not to the families, given that its success is dependent on a code word. In the event that a child is attempted to be forcibly removed from the care of the center by an individual who is not authorized to have custody of the child, the following procedures will be followed:

- The child's teacher will be alerted of the emergency situation through a designated code word followed by the child's name.
- The teacher will calmly take the child into a room that can lock from the inside. This will be the designated safe place.
- If the individual who called the alert is able to reach a phone, he or she will place a call to 911. If this individual is not able to reach the phone, he or she will assign another teacher to make the call.
- The teacher and child will remain inside the locked room until the police arrive at the center.
- The remaining children in the class will be monitored by another staff member until the teacher is able to return.
- All these procedures should be done as quickly and calmly as possible in an attempt to prevent the person attempting abduction from locating the child and removing him or her from the center.

The staff members of your center should also be presented with a confidentiality policy. Child care professionals respect families', children's, and colleagues' privacy. Your staff should be aware that information shared within the child care center is regarded as sacred and confidential. When confidentiality is not respected, misunderstandings, hurt feelings, shattered relationships, and broken laws result. Repeating information that is sensitive damages the self-esteem of children and colleagues. Putting this information into a policy format and distributing it to staff members can impress upon them how important confidentiality is and their duty to uphold it.

Welcome Pack

We have reviewed a variety of policies and procedures that can be effectively communicated by using handouts. In order for your communication to be successful, you will need to develop a method for presenting the information to your audience. One way to do so is to create a Welcome Pack, which is distributed to all families at the time of enrollment or, if they are returning families, at the time their child's program commences. The Welcome Pack should be placed in a folder or other paper containment device so the information can easily be stored together for future reference. In addition to including your handbook you should also include all important policy and procedure handouts. At the start of the school year, Parent Packs can be tailored for individual programs by including program-specific newsletters and calendars.

Beginnings can be fraught with anxiety and uncertainty, you can help to alleviate some of these fears through adequate preparation. Included in the Welcome Pack should be the welcome letter, calendar, tuition rate schedule, handbook, and important policy handouts.

The welcome letter will serve as the first formal introduction to newly enrolled families and sets the communication tone for the year. This should be mailed to new families several weeks in advance of the program beginning. If the family has joined your center in the middle of the year, the Welcome Packet should be provided to the family at the time of enrollment but in advance of the child's first day. The letter should strive for a polished and professional tone and should include the relevant information your families will need to prepare their child for the first day at your center. Begin your letter by warmly welcoming your new family and reiterate how pleased you are that they have chosen your center. Then confirm which program they have registered their child in and the time and date their specific program begins. It is also useful to reinforce center opening and closing times so that families can appropriately schedule drop-offs and pickups.

Next, let your families know what they should do upon arrival at your center. Will someone be available to greet them at the door and show them to the appropriate learning area? Should they look for posted classroom lists and area assignments? By providing your families with specific information, you will be decreasing the level of confusion and apprehension for both families and children.

A smooth transition can set the tone for a positive first day. Some families may also wish to visit your center with their child prior to the start of the program. If feasible, allow new children to look around, explore the environment, and play with some of the toys while their family remains close by. This "dress rehearsal" may help the child feel more comfortable at your center on their first day. The transition may also be easier if the children can attend the center for a shortened day without their families remaining at the center. These possibilities should be presented to families in your welcome letter.

Also included in the welcome letter should be a checklist of items your families will need to bring with them on the first day. Typically these include: naptime items, a

WHEN COMMUNICATION BREAKS DOWN

FAMILY: "My child is supposed to be starting the three-year-old program today but the classroom teacher just told me that I cannot leave him without a completed physical form. He has an appointment with the pediatrician tomorrow, I did not think that would be a problem. My child has been looking forward to this day for months and is going to be really upset that he cannot stay and play with the other kids. Can't you make an exception and let him stay today? I will bring the completed physical form in tomorrow."

STAFF: "I am sorry but according to state regulations all children must have a completed physical before they can enter the classroom. We cannot make any exceptions to this law. Your child will not be able to attend the program today."

COMMUNICATION LESSON: New families may not understand that certain items are required by law prior to entering a child care center. Since your families will have differing levels of familiarity with what is required of them, it is the responsibility of the center to educate new families on their responsibilities. This should be done well in advance of the first day of school in order to prevent confusion and disappointment on the part of your families and their children.

lunch box with icepack, extra clothing, and completed registration and medical forms. If this is a family's first experience with a child care center, they may be unaware of all of the preparation needed for the first day of school. A comprehensive checklist will help to ensure that all families arrive at the center adequately prepared.

Activity 6.3 Creating a Welcome Letter

Using the template provided on page 100, customize a welcome letter for each of your programs.

Welcome Letter Template

Print this form from the enclosed CD!

Dear Families,

Our staff would like to welcome you to our [name of program here].

[Center name] begins at [opening time] and closes by [closing time]. Your child may be dropped off and picked up any time between these hours.

[Program name] begins on [date program starts]. Class and area assignments will be posted on the first day in our center lobby window. Our teachers and administrators will be available this week to assist your family and answer any questions you may have about the start of school. We want you and your family to feel comfortable. Feel free to stop by any time during the remainder of the summer for a visit. Families can look around, play with toys, visit our bathrooms, and explore our environment.

What to know:

- All families must sign in and out of our center. Please make us aware of any alternate people picking up your child. We will require they bring photo ID.
- We ask that everyone read our sick policy before entering our center. Please notify our staff of any allergies or medical issues regarding your child.
- Stop by our Parent Information Table. Handbooks, curriculum guides, policy statements, school calendars, and other important information will be available.

What to bring (label all items with child's name):

- Items for naptime: A crib sheet, small pillow, and blanket may be used. Your child's favorite stuffed animal is optional. You must bring all nap items home to wash at the end of each week.
- Lunch box with ice pack. This center is a peanut-free school. Please read all labels to ensure that you do not send your child to school with any peanut-containing products. An ice pack must be placed in each lunch box, regardless of the contents.
- Extra clothing to be kept at our center. Please bring a shirt, pants, two pairs of underwear, and socks.
- Toys from home are optional. Children may bring one small toy from home. Home toys can be taken out only at designated times. Our center has lots of toys, manipulatives, blocks, dress-up items, and so on. . . . Many engaging activities and hands-on lessons are planned daily, therefore, toys from home are not necessary.

Please check that you have the following items:

☐ Completed enrollment form
- Current address, home phone no., workplace phone no., cell phone no.
- Doctor and dentist phone nos.
- Two emergency pickups and phone nos.
- Authorized signature located on bottom of form

☐ Completed emergency card

☐ Current physical exam including any allergies, medications, or medical needs

We hope your family is as excited as we are to begin school!
We look forward to spending time with you!

Program Calendar

Attached to the welcome letter should be the calendar for the program. The annual calendar should detail the days your center will be closed or will otherwise deviate from normal center hours. If your center has multiple programs, you should create a calendar specifically tailored to each program. Centers that have distinct programs for the academic year versus the summer should create separate calendars for each program. Once you have published the days and hours your center will be operating, you must abide by the calendar. Your families depend on your center and can be affected by unexpected schedule changes. If your center has any special events, such as a holiday program or graduation ceremony, these should also be included on the calendar whenever practical. This additional level of detail will help your families to plan vacations, notify employers of days they will need off, and make arrangements for alternative child care when the center is closed.

The calendar should be easy to read and attractively presented so your families will post it in a prominent spot in their household where it can be referred to often. A copy of the calendar should also be prominently displayed on a conspicuously placed bulletin board at the center (Chapter 7 will discuss appropriate center visuals in detail).

The second attachment to the welcome letter should be the tuition rate schedule for the program. Your handbook provides families with information regarding the due dates for tuition payments and penalties for late payments. However, since the specific tuition rate is likely to change on an annual basis, this information is more appropriately communicated through a handout. It is prudent to include an effective date as a footnote to this page, as well as a notation that tuition is subject to change.

Your Welcome Packet has established the first formal communication to your families through handouts. Your center should continue to utilize this method of communication to keep your families well informed on updated center policies and other pertinent information not covered in the handbook.

ACTIVITY 6.4 Creating a Program-Specific Calendar

Using the template provided on page 102, create a calendar that provides your families with the dates your center will be closed, will be closing early, or will be holding special events. Calendars should be printed on brightly colored paper so they are easily recognizable, you may also want to consider laminating the calendar so it can withstand an entire year of use.

Program-Specific Calendar Template

Print this form from the enclosed CD!

Half Day Preschool Calendar 2003–2004			
August	Th F	28 29	Open House—3's A.M. & P.M. Programs Open House—4's A.M. & P.M. & Enrich. Programs
September	M T W	1 2 3	Labor Day—Center is closed Welcome to 3's and 4's (M–F) Enrichment Programs Welcome to 4's (M, W, F) Programs
October	M Th, F M TBA	6 9, 10 13 	Yom Kippur—No Half-Day Preschool No Public School—No Half-Day Preschool Columbus Day—No Half–Day Preschool Parent Orientation Night ***Parent attendance is highly recommended**
November	T W–F	11 26–28	Veterans Day—No Half-Day Preschool Thanksgiving Break—No Half-Day Preschool
December	W–W	24–31	Holiday Vacation—No Half-Day Preschool

*During winter months listen to the radio or watch your local TV station for public school closings. *Half-day preschool will not be held on public school snow days.* Half-day preschool is unaffected by morning public school *delays* and will run classes at regular scheduled times.

January	Th F F M	1 2 16 19	New Year's Day—Center is closed Holiday Vacation—No Half-Day Preschool Public School Staff Devel. Day–No Half-Day Preschool Martin Luther King Day—No Half-Day Preschool
February	M, T	16,17	Presidents' Weekend—No Half-Day Preschool
March			
April	F M–F TBA	9 19–23 	Good Friday—Center is *closed* Spring Vacation—No Half-Day Preschool 4's Program Parent-Teacher Conferences
May	M TBA	31 	Memorial Day—Center is *closed* 3's Program Parent-Teacher Conferences
June	F TBA	11 	Tentative Final Day of Half-Day Preschool End of the year Graduation Picnic

Program Curriculum

Your handbook has provided your families with a basic outline of the curricula they can expect from each program. However, once their child is enrolled in the program, your families will expect more detailed information as to the types of skills their child is working on each week. There are several methods of providing this information to your families. Curricula should be presented to your families on both a macro and micro level. At the start of the school year, families can be presented with a handout describing what their child will be learning over the course of the year. This curricula should coincide with the one presented in the handbook for each program. However, the handout should provide more details about the specific types of activities the children will be exposed to in order to foster their social, emotional, and intellectual growth.

You have likely spent a great deal of time preparing your curriculum and supporting activities. A well thought out curriculum is at the heart of every great child care center. The curriculum handout will introduce the fundamentals of your center's approach to learning, so you should ensure that it is both well organized and comprehensive. The amount of information presented to children over the course of a year can seem overwhelming, so you will need to structure your handout so that the information delivered will be easily comprehended by all of your families.

When you have an abundance of information to communicate, it is often prudent to dissect the message into several smaller and more manageable groups. In terms of curriculum, the yearly objectives can be divided by subject manner. Your curriculum handout can be structured to address the topics of mathematics, language arts, reading (or reading readiness), social studies, science, music, art, and physical education. Within each of the curriculum categories, you can address the major objectives of your center's program. You can ensure that each concept is understood by providing a concrete example of how the children in your program will be encouraged to meet the objective. For example, if one of the objectives listed under music was to "promote coordination and self-expression through music," you could provide the example of using audiotapes that promote moving to music and rhythm.

ACTIVITY 6.5 Creating a Program Curriculum

Review the curriculum example provided. Using the example given, design a curriculum that provides your families with the types of skills their child will be exposed to over the school year. You should aim to list at least five objectives under each learning category and provide examples to clarify specific objectives. The curriculum outline will have to be adjusted in order to be age appropriate for the program.

Sample Preschool Curriculum

Language Arts

(Three-Year-Old Half-day Curriculum)

* Beginning writing skills
   Upper- & Lowercase
* Alphabet Skills
   Letter Recognition
   Letter Sounds
* Literature/Nursery Rhymes
* Tracing

Math Skills

(Four-Year-Old Enrichment Curriculum)

* Simple addition
* Measuring/Volume
* Number Recognition
* Estimating
* Size
* Counting
* Categorizing
* Shapes
* Concept of Zero
* Patterns
* Sequencing
* Spatial Relations

Classroom Skills

(Four-Year-Old Full-day Curriculum)

* Social Skills
* Independence Skills
* Practical Life Skills
* Scissors Skills
* Fine & Gross Motor Skills
* Listening
* Following Directions

Social Studies

(Four-Year-Old Half-day Curriculum)

* Family and Friends
* Holidays
* Child Safety
* Transportation
* Daily Calendar
* Days/Months/Years
* Community Helpers
* Manners
* Cooperation
* All About Me
* Fire Prevention
* World Cultures
* Feelings/Emotions
* Communication
* Physically Challenged

The [center] has developed separate written curricula for each program at our center. Our teachers plan lessons within the framework of the curriculum and have appropriate materials at their disposal. The scope and intensity of our curricula accelerate as our children grow. Parents are given copies of their child's curriculum and receive weekly notices of the next week's activities.

Music & Movement

(Both Three- and Four-Year-Old Curriculum)

* Instruments
* Rhythm
* Sounds—loud and soft
* Singing
* Dancing
* Parachute Play
* Gross Motor Games
* Beanbag Play
   Music from around the
   Globe
* CDs
* Obstacle Courses

Arts & Crafts

(Three-Year-Old Full-day Curriculum)

* Sculpting: Clay
            Putty
* Painting: Tampera Paints
            Watercolors
* Drawing: Pencil
            Crayon
            Markers
            Chalks
* Creating: Glue
            Glitter
            Fabrics
            Papers
            Feathers
            Nature materials

(This is one component of our Kindergarten Language Arts Curriculum. Other areas included are handwriting, writing listening skills, and oral skills.)

Literature:

* Show enthusiasm for a variety of literature (folk tales, nursery rhymes, fantasy, etc.).
* Discuss the setting, details, and characters of a story or poem.
* Discuss favorite parts or ideas generated by stories or poems.
* Show an understanding of a variety of illustrations in books (i.e., watercolor, line drawing, etc.)
* Support a personal evaluation of a story (I like it because . . .).

EFFECTIVE COMMUNICATION IN ACTION

FAMILY: "I am concerned that Tommy is not able to identify colors yet. Do you think that there could be something wrong with his eyes?"

PLAN FOR COMMUNICATION:
1. Identify the concern of the family.
2. Suggest potential solutions.

STAFF: "If you have any reason to suspect a medical problem I would definately suggest that you take Tommy to a physician for a checkup. However, it is not unusual for a child of Tommy's age not to know his colors yet. I would suggest that you work with him at home. You can take a look at our curriculum calendar, which will tell you what skills we will be working on in the classroom each month. When we get to color skills, you can work color identification into your everyday activities. When driving to school, point out blue houses or red cars. The more Tommy hears these words, the more familiar the concepts will become. Please let me know if you have any questions as you review the curricula. You can also expect more detailed descriptions of our lesson plans in the weekly Coming Attractions newsletter."

Attached to the curricula you should include a calendar that provides information about which lessons will be covered during which months. You do not need to give details here—the details will come in the form of weekly newsletters. For example, in preparing a monthly kindergarten curriculum, you may include the introduction of the letters A–G in September, H–M in October, N–R in November, and S–Z in December. These brief time lines will allow your families to better understand the flow of the curriculum, and if they wish, help their child prepare for the upcoming units.

Newsletters

With your welcome pack you have taken the first step in proactively establishing communication with the families of the center. In order to keep the lines of communication open you will need to use newsletters in addition to your handouts. We will be discussing several types of newsletters, weekly Coming Attractions, Health Alerts, Tuition Reminders, and Director's Newsletters, which can serve as valuable communication tools.

ACTIVITY 6.6 Creating a Coming Attractions Newsletter

Using the template provided on page 107, create a newsletter that informs families of the activities that will be performed over the following week. Consideration should be given to any materials the child will need to bring from home as well as the skills that each activity will be promoting.

Coming Attractions

One of the most useful and eagerly anticipated newsletters is one that previews the activities for the next week. This newsletter can be entitled "Coming Attractions" and should be developed individually by each teacher. For each day of the program, specific activities should be listed as well as the skill each activity will be developing. Providing families with this information not only demonstrates adherence to the curriculum, it also allows children to show up for school each day appropriately dressed for the planned activities and gives families a chance to reinforce at home the lessons learned at the center. The Coming Attractions newsletters should be prepared by the individual teachers two weeks in advance and provided to the head teacher or director for review. They should be distributed to the families one week in advance so families can be active participants in their child's learning.

Health Alerts

The health and safety of the children in your care should be a concern of paramount importance. The child care environment is highly conducive to contagious infections. It is impossible to eliminate illness at your center, but you can attempt to diminish its effects by reminding your families of the sick child policy. If one child comes to your center with a contagious disease, all of the other children in your center are put at risk. Your families have a responsibility to the other children in the center to carefully monitor their child's health and to report to the center if their child becomes ill.

Despite your best efforts, it is often inevitable that a child attends the center during the course of a contagious infection. Once a family reports that their child has been diagnosed with a contagious illness, you will need to decide whether it is prudent to inform other families. Many centers use a newsletter format of Health Alert notices to communicate possible exposure to families. These Health Alerts should be posted in a conspicuous place at the center (appropriate placement will be discussed further in Chapter 7), and should be written in a nonalarmist and informative manner. It is important to protect the privacy of the family who initially reported the illness. Your center should never disclose the name of the child who contracted the illness or the

Coming Attractions Newsletter Template

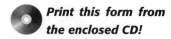
Print this form from the enclosed CD!

Coming Attractions

Half-Day Fours
Enrichment

Week _____

Teacher _____

Theme: _____   Skill: _____

MONDAY

TUESDAY

WEDNESDAY

THURSDAY

FRIDAY

Science Topic   Weekly Reader Day   Computer Day

NOTES FROM THE TEACHER:

classroom the child was assigned to. Included in the Health Alert should be the name of the reported infection, information on symptoms of infection, the approximate incubation period, what the center is doing to contain the spread of infection, and the recommended course of action if symptoms are detected in a child.

Since infection can spread rapidly and some advance preparation is needed to ensure the accuracy of the information contained within the Health Alerts, it is prudent to draft Health Alerts for the most commonly experienced infections in advance. For example, your center should be prepared to handle reports of head lice, strep throat, pink eye, and chicken pox. Your local pediatrician's office can be a useful source of information in your preparation of Health Alerts. Most offices will have on hand informational packets on the most common childhood illnesses, and you can use these resources to provide families with accurate and complete information in your Health Alerts.

The purpose of Health Alerts is to provide your families with information, not to help them make medical judgments. Unless you are a medical professional you should refer all families with questions to a local physician or nurse.

Tuition Reminders

In order for your center to operate successfully, you must rely on on-time tuition payments. Issues related to money can be uncomfortable to broach with your families. You can use newsletters to help you communicate with your families in cases of delinquent tuition payments. With all of the daily activities your families are involved in, it is not uncommon for a payment to be forgotten. In these cases, a gentle reminder may be all that is needed. It is also possible that a payment was made but was inadvertently not recorded by your center. This newsletter should have a friendly, cooperative tone. You want to avoid confrontation while still acknowledging that the missed payment needs to be made.

ACTIVITY 6.7 Creating Effective Health Alerts: Lice

Provided on page 109 is a template of a Health Alert designed to inform families about head lice. Using the template, create additional Health Alerts for strep throat and chicken pox. You should have these reviewed by a medical professional for completeness and accuracy before the information is disseminated to your families.

Health Alert Template

Print this form from the enclosed CD!

Health Alert

It has recently been reported to the center that your child may have been exposed to head lice.

What it is:

Head lice are insects that live in human hair and can cause extreme itching. It is important to remember that anyone can get head lice and that, although the itching can be uncomfortable, *they are not dangerous* to your child.

How it is spread:

- Using an infested comb or brush
- Hanging your coat or hat next to an infested item
- Resting your head on upholstered furniture or a pillow recently used by an infested person
- Direct head-to-head contact

What to look for:

- Excessive itching or scratching of the head
- Examine the hair and scalp for white or grayish crawling forms (about the size of a sesame seed) and yellowish white eggs (nits) attached to the hair shafts close to the scalp. You should be able to see these with the naked eye.
- Red bite marks or scratch marks are often seen on the scalp or neck.

What you can do:

- Examine your child's head carefully every night.
- Bring home your child's nap items and launder them in hot soapy water.
- Launder all hats, toys, and coats that may have been brought into the center.

If you suspect your child has been infected:

- Call your child's pediatrician for recommendation on treatment
- Call the center to report the infestation
- Your child may not return to the center until the infestation has been cleared and no nits are visible in the hair.

What we are doing to prevent the spread:

- All fabric toys and items in the dress-up area have been laundered.
- All nap cots have been disinfected.
- All coats and hats will be stored in separate cubbies.

ACTIVITY 6.8 Creating a Friendly Payment Reminder

Use the template provided below to customize a reminder that notifies a family that an expected tuition payment has been missed. These reminders should be placed in a location where it is visible only to the family it is intended for.

Payment Reminder Template

Print this form from the enclosed CD!

A FRIENDLY REMINDER

Level One Notice   Date: _____

Fee Due: _____   **For the Week of:** _____

We do not have a record of your payment. Has it been overlooked? Please stop by the office to make your payment. The above fee due includes a late fee of $10.00. If this payment has already been made, please stop by and let us know on what day it was made so we can properly credit your account.

Thank you for your cooperation!

If you do not see any action as a result of the first reminder, you will need to take more definitive steps. The second letter to a family alerting them to a late payment should be issued within two weeks of the missed payment. This letter should have a more formal tone than the previous reminder. If your center has an established policy for delinquent tuition, it should be stated in this letter. The letter should also delineate the time frame within which the family must bring their account up to date and the consequences of not doing so.

Director's Newsletter

The director of the center has a responsibility for keeping the families informed regarding the center happenings and making him- or herself available for questions and comments. One way to ensure that regular communication occurs between a director and a family is by publishing a Director's Newsletter. The newsletter can address issues pertinent to the center, policies, upcoming special events, or introduction of new staff members. The content could also be issues that concern all families, not just the ones affiliated with the center. Topics can be seasonally appropriate, such as pool safety in the June newsletter and preparing your kids for going back to school in September. You can ask the children in your center to help decorate the newsletter by providing artwork or puzzles to be included on the pages. The director can offer individual teachers opportunities to become involved as well. Each newsletter can spotlight one teacher and the special activities ongoing in his or her classroom. The newsletter should be structured in such a manner that the director is portrayed as involved, concerned, and approachable.

Handouts and newsletters are effective ways to notify your families about a variety of important issues. They should be structured in such a way that they are informative without being overwhelming and should be as brief as possible. Although they can easily reach large audiences quickly, it should be noted that they can never take the place of face-to-face interaction. A handout or newsletter that covers information that may be distressing or confusing to your families should always be followed with an in-person consultation.

Communication Progress Report

Skill or Task	Range of Abilities		
	ALWAYS MEET	EMERGING SKILL	WILL IMPROVE
Information to be presented to families is always done in the most appropriate method—handout, handbook, or newsletter.	☐	☐	☐
A comprehensive welcome packet has been established.	☐	☐	☐
Families arriving at the center on the first day are adequately prepared as a result of the welcome packet.	☐	☐	☐
The annual calendar is easy to use and attractively presented.	☐	☐	☐
Families are able to determine important dates from the calendar.	☐	☐	☐
Curriculum handouts coincide with what has been presented in the handbook.	☐	☐	☐
Curriculum has been divided into easy to manage sections with specific examples given for learning objectives.	☐	☐	☐
Health Alerts have been prepared for the most common illnesses.	☐	☐	☐
Health Alerts have been reviewed by a medical professional for accuracy.	☐	☐	☐
Two levels of tuition reminders have been created for use as handouts in the event of delinquent tuition.	☐	☐	☐
All handouts are informative without providing unneeded information.	☐	☐	☐
Families know where to turn if they require additional information.	☐	☐	☐

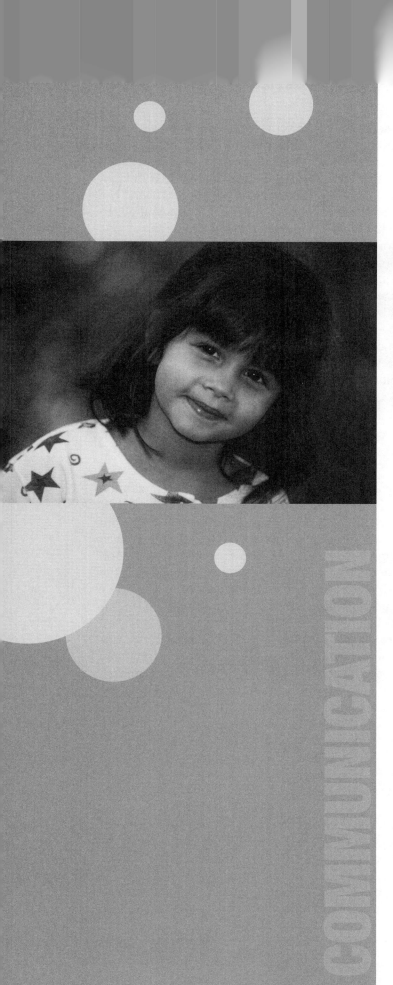

Projecting the Right Image: A Look at Visual Communication

COMING ATTRACTIONS

- How to make your center stand out

- How to design materials that will be immediately recognized as belonging to your center

- How to use visually appealing tools to enhance communication between your center and your families

COMMUNICATION

In previous chapters we have discussed written and verbal communication with your audiences. We will now turn our attention to visual communication techniques, an approach that is often overlooked. Each time people enter the doors of your center, they are immediately confronted with a multitude of images. The materials contained within the entryway, the layout of the classrooms, the disposition of your staff, and the faces of the children are all visual clues to the type of environment they are about to enter. Each one of your five target audiences (current students and families, staff, potential students and families, neighbors, and vendors) will be looking for something different. Current families will look for an environment that feels friendly and welcoming. Your staff members will look for job satisfaction, advancement opportunities, and excitement. New or potential families will look for visual confirmation of a professional and trustworthy center. Neighbors and vendors will look for organization and commitment to the community. All of these needs can be met if your center carefully plans and implements a specific image. You can communicate a positive and professional image through the use of a logo, name tags, letterhead, t-shirts and hats, student "mailboxes," motivational charts, awards and diplomas, bulletin boards, staff biographies, scrapbooks, a family resource library, and a suggestion box.

Logo

The development of a logo provides your center and the materials associated with the center with a way to be easily recognized by your audiences. A logo is usually symbolic or pictorial in nature and may have components of the center name incorporated within it. You will want to design a logo that is simple enough that it can be easily reproduced on a multitude of materials, including letterhead, newspaper advertisements, and t-shirts, but unique enough that your audiences will be able to immediately connect the image to your center. Your logo will also make a statement about your center. The colors and designs used can project a multitude of images, from young and playful to serious and academic. The development of a logo is a process that will require a significant amount of thought and research. Once developed, a logo should remain with the center throughout the lifespan of the business. When developing something so permanent, you want to ensure that you have the best possible product before finalizing the design.

The search for a logo can begin with the people who know your center the best, the staff members and students. You can ask both your staff and students to design a picture they feel captures the spirit of the center. Obviously, when dealing with small children you will have to communicate the task in very basic terms, such as, "Draw a picture that shows what you like best at school." You may be surprised at the ability of your students and staff to effectively convey their feelings about the center through pictures. Even if this exercise does not produce the design you are looking for, it can be a very inspiring and informative activity.

A logo can be designed in black and white or can have color incorporated. In keeping with the tone of simplicity, most logos contain only one or two colors. These colors can then become your signature, and you can use them to further identify your center. For example, if you choose a certain shade of blue for your logo, you should try to incorporate the same color into your marketing and advertising materials, handouts and newsletters, and any promotional gifts given to your families or staff. During field trips or special events you can also request that the staff and students wear t-shirts or hats in that color so they are easily recognizable as a group.

Name Tags

Name tags are not only a useful way to convey professionalism and facilitate communication, they are also an important feature in helping to maintain safety and security within the center. Your staff members should always be easily identifiable to families and children. Wearing a name tag is any easy way to accomplish this. The name tag should identify the staff member in the manner he or she wishes to be addressed. For example, if your teachers are addressed by children and their families by their first names, the name tag should identify the staff member by first and last name. If you prefer your staff members to be addressed formally using Mr., Mrs., or Ms., these prefixes should also be added to the name tag. A family member who is unable to remember the name of their child's teacher or is unsure how they should be addressed may be anxious about approaching the staff member. Through the use of name tags, this anxiety is circumvented. A name tag also provides visual confirmation of which adults belong in the classroom. If each staff member and authorized visitor is required to wear an identifying name tag, recognizing individuals who do not have permission to be in the classroom becomes an easy task.

You can add a personal touch to each name tag by implementing a system that identifies the number of years a staff member has been affiliated with your center. For example, attaching a piece of felt to a name tag allows you to hang small decorations that correspond to the number of years a teacher has been at the center. You will likely need two different types of decorations, one representing one year of service and one representing five years, to cover all possible combinations. For example, if a silver pencil is given to denote one year of service and a golden apple means five years, a teacher whose name tag displays one gold apple and two silver pencils has been employed by the center for seven years. This simple gesture serves as a recognizable reward for your most loyal staff members and can be a conversation starter for children and their families. You incorporate the annual distribution of ornaments into a staff appreciation ceremony. Families should also receive a handout explaining the significance of the name tag decorations and an example of how to calculate the number of years a staff member has been with the center.

Name tags are a necessity for adults visiting the classroom, whether they are family members or outside vendors. Your staff members should be trained to question any adult within the classroom who is not properly identified. Name tags for visitors can be easily constructed using generic, store-purchased name tags or can be made more permanent using lamination. Each visitor receives a name tag when he or she stops by the office to register. Any permanent visitor name tags should be returned prior to the visitor leaving the center. The center should be aware of how many visitor name tags are available and should make sure all are accounted for on a daily basis.

Name tags can also be useful in early teacher-student communications. During the first week of school, name tags are useful tools for the teacher to learn the names of the students and for the children to learn the place of their personal spaces. A student name tag can be decorated with a picture that corresponds to a picture found on the cubby, mailbox, and lunch box space. Although preschool children are unable to read, you can use picture recognition as a way to promote independence and a sense of autonomy over their belongings. Student name tags can be extremely useful inside the classroom, however, it is important to note that for safety reasons, they should always be removed prior to the children leaving the center. Small children can be tricked into believing someone who knows their name is not a stranger. This concept should also be taught to families so that names placed on bags and lunch boxes are not easily read by a passerby.

Letterhead

The use of letterhead not only gives your important documents a professional appearance, it also allows for immediate recognition of the document's source. Your logo should be incorporated into your letterhead, as should the name of the center. Many centers also choose to have the center address and phone number printed onto the letterhead so this contact information is readily available should the reader have questions. In the child care setting it is not necessary for every newsletter or handout to be printed on letterhead, as some of the more creative and casual documents are better suited to standard paper. However, for important written communication with your audiences, letterhead is an extra touch that can make a positive impression on the reader. You should also consider printing your logo and name on other necessary elements of business communication, such as envelopes, folders, and business cards. A Welcome Pack that is presented in a folder professionally printed with the name and logo of the center can appear to your audience to be more well thought out and polished than one that is simply stapled together. The use of professional letterhead and other business supplies can be costly, and you will need to weigh the benefits against the cost. Prior to making an investment in professional printing, your center can use clip art and other graphic design programs to give a professional feel to your correspondence. While business stationery may not be of paramount importance to a new, growing operation, it is almost always a necessity for large, well-established child care centers.

T-Shirts and Hats

Logos are not for paper documents alone. They can also be printed on name tags, hats, t-shirts, water bottles, pens, and hundreds of other items for everyday use. Families like to be given a token of your appreciation, and a gift of a hat or t-shirt bearing the center logo and name is a way to thank your families while simultaneously providing advertisement for your center. When the children travel in groups outside the center, an identifiable t-shirt or hat can also help the teacher quickly identify the children he or she is responsible for. You do not need to choose the highest quality materials for your items, as they are often quickly outgrown or succumb to the damages of child play. If professionally printed t-shirts are too great of an investment for your center at this time, you can consider purchasing plain t-shirts in your center's color and decorating them with the children.

Student "Mailboxes"

Your handouts and newsletters will only be effective if your center has implemented a system for ensuring that your families receive all communication from the center in a timely and confidential manner. This is one of the most crucial steps in communication with your current families, but it is also one of the most easily accomplished. Each student can be given a mailbox, consisting of a large manila envelope and decorated with his or her name and picture. The mailboxes should be grouped together by classroom and placed securely in a mailbox holder (as shown) so the contents cannot be easily disrupted or dislodged.

The center staff is responsible for placing any handouts or newsletters into the student mailbox, along with any artwork or projects completed throughout the course of the day. Families will need to check the mailbox each day their child is at the center and take home the contents. The mailbox holders should be located in a place that is easily accessible to families and does not require intervention on the part of the teacher to access the materials. It is also important to keep the area looking neat and organized. You will need to limit the number of mailboxes in each mailbox holder to ensure that the materials placed within them do not become compromised by lack of space.

Involving the children in the process is a great way to ensure that all materials placed within the mailboxes are actually received and reviewed by your families. The picture on a child's name tag and cubby can also be placed above the class mailbox holder. Most young children are able to recognize their own picture and should be

Example of Child's Mailbox

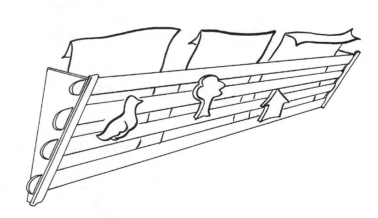

Example of Mailbox Holder

able to distinguish their mailbox from ones belonging to other children. Upon completion of a special project, you can ask the children to place it inside their mailbox. For this reason, you will need to ensure that the mailbox holders have been securely anchored to the wall at a height that is easily accessible for young children. The extra bit of involvement on the part of the children makes it more likely that they will run to their mailboxes to show off their treasures when families arrive for pickup time. In addition to collecting the child's projects, the families will also be receiving the important handouts and newsletters.

Since student mailboxes are the most commonly used form of communication with your families, you will want to ensure that they are well maintained. Mailboxes that are opened multiple times a day may start to show signs of wear and tear. Any mailbox with significant damage should be replaced, which, given the economical design of the mailboxes, should not be a burden on the center, even if it needs to be done on several occasions throughout the year. You can decrease the need for regular replacement of mailboxes by reminding families that the mailboxes need to stay within the center (families who remove the mailbox along with the contents at the end of the day are likely to forget to return it).

Motivational Charts

Most child care centers adhere to a specific schedule that is followed throughout the day. Although the daily activities may vary, the flow of the day remains constant. You can use this set schedule to communicate with families regarding their child's behavior throughout the course of the day. A motivational chart helps to break down the day into specific time frames; such as drop-off, lunch time, outside play time, and naptime. Each day a child should receive a new motivational chart. At the completion of each time frame, the teacher will put a sticker on the chart if the child successfully completed that portion of the day. The determination of successful completion can be based on a number of parameters, such as positive interactions or appropriate behavior, depending on the activity. At the end of the day, the motivational chart will be placed in the child's mailbox for the family to review. Children are often proud of their accomplishments throughout the day and eager to show off the stickers they received to their families. The motivational chart also helps families and teachers identify the transitions during the day where the child has room for continued growth and development. Working together, the family and teacher can support the child in their acquisition of new skills.

ACTIVITY 7.1 Creating a Daily Motivational Chart

Using the template provided on page 119, customize the motivational chart to fit the daily activities of your program. Since each day is a chance for a fresh start, completed charts should be given to your families at the end of the day and a new one begun the following morning.

🖸 **Print this form from the enclosed CD!**

Motivational Chart

Drop-Off Time

Calendar Time

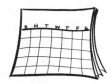

Snack Time

Outside Time

Art/Science/Readiness Time

Pickup Time

Awards and Diplomas

Everyone enjoys having their accomplishments recognized, and children are no exception to this rule. Each child in your center will bring a unique set of abilities and interests, and as a child care professional, one of your duties is to learn about the interests of the children in your care and use those interests as motivational tools for learning. Acceptance and recognition of special qualities and talents can make a profound difference in the self-esteem of a developing child. It is also important to share with your families the accomplishments of their children on a regular basis. While family-teacher conferences, which will be discussed in depth in Chapter 8, are the formal venue for progress reports, families appreciate more frequent but less formal acknowledgments that their child is growing and learning during the hours in your care. An easy way to communicate everyday accomplishments to families is through the use of awards.

Awards can be given for a wide variety of activities and accomplishments. As your children complete the skills listed on your curriculum, you can notify their families with an award of achievement or recognition. The awards can be designed using clip art or pictures made by the children and should be signed by the teacher. In addition to scholastic achievements, it is also important to recognize developmental milestones. For example, children deserve recognition for the first time they are able to tie their shoes alone. If the first time occurs at your center, you will want to make sure that the child's family is notified of the event so they can also offer their praise at home. When children's accomplishments are rewarded, they are often more eager to attempt new skills.

The children are not the only audience who deserves recognition. Family members who volunteer their time to spend time with the children, either through a Helping Hands program or field trip (both which will be discussed in detail in Chapter 9), can have their efforts recognized through an award. Vendors who contribute generously to the center should also be recognized. The actual award or certificate of appreciation does not have to be professionally developed; this is one area where it truly is the thought that counts. This is also a valuable step in building a positive relationship with a member of your communication audience.

ACTIVITY 7.2 Designing a Certificate of Accomplishment for Children

Using the template provided on page 121, design certificates that can be presented to children to celebrate their accomplishments. There are endless possibilities for actions that merit recognition. Here are some suggestions: tying own shoes, losing first tooth, completing potty training, making specific letters/numbers, learning to write their name, knowing own phone number, recognizing colors, ability to recite days of the week, being a good friend, helping the teacher, taking care of the classroom pets, or being a good listener.

Child's Certificate of Accomplishment Template

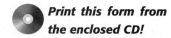

I CAN WRITE MY NAME!

Date:

ACTIVITY 7.3 Designing a Certificate of Accomplishment for Adults

Using the template provided on page 122, design certificates that can be presented to adults who have contributed to your classroom. Vendors who have contributed free materials or time or family members who have enriched the classroom experience for the children deserve to have their efforts acknowledged.

Adult Certificate of Accomplishment Template

Print this form from the enclosed CD!

THANK YOU

for taking the
time to show us your
fire truck and
equipment.

Sincerely,
The Staff

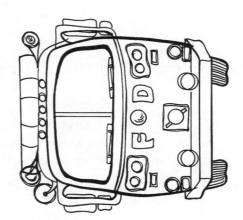

Completing an academic year or program is an accomplishment at any age. You can officially commemorate this milestone by awarding diplomas to your students. The diploma should be designed in a way that it accentuates the unique qualities of your center. One of the best ways to do this is to involve the children in the development of their diploma. Children can design artwork to create a border around the diploma, or they can work together to choose one picture which they would like to see on the diploma. The logo of the center should be included on the diploma as should the signature of the classroom teacher. A few extra details such as color or lamination can make the diploma a piece of artwork that can be displayed in the family home for years to come. In the case of significant milestones, such as graduation from preschool, the diploma can be presented at a graduation ceremony. (Details of the graduation ceremony will be discussed in Chapter 9.)

Bulletin Boards

Bulletin boards, like mailboxes, are low-tech but effective ways to communicate with each person who enters the center. They show advance planning and organization on the part of the center and allow families to become involved in their child's learning activities. The placement of bulletin boards will be dependent on the audience you intend the contents to reach. There are typically three types of bulletin boards within a center, those that are center wide, those that are program specific, and those that are staff specific. A bulletin board placed in the entryway of your center will be seen by all who enter, while one dealing specifically with staffing information should be placed in an area easily accessible to your staff but not your families. The purpose of each bulletin board is to provide an easy way for the audience to access important information. The information chosen for a bulletin board is typically important in nature and should have previously appeared in an individual handout or newsletter. If the individual notice was inadvertently missed, a bulletin board provides your audiences a second opportunity to receive the information.

A bulletin board located in the entry of your school is an ideal place to post information about all of your different programs. For example, the annual calendars for all programs and the dates and times the center will be closed early are handouts that belong on a center-wide bulletin board. Families of one program are able to learn about the activities of other programs that may be a good fit for their child at a later date or may be of interest to their friends and neighbors with children. Potential families entering the center are able to see the variety of programs they have to choose from for their child and the scheduling difference between the programs. Special works of art from children of all ages can also be displayed on the center-wide bulletin board to increase its visual appeal. In order for the bulletin board to serve as a useful communication tool, it must be kept current and uncluttered. If you have multiple staff members, the responsibility of bulletin board maintenance should be overseen by one individual who has communicated with all other staff members on the necessary content of the board.

A Well-Organized Bulletin Board Designed to Provide Families with General Center Information

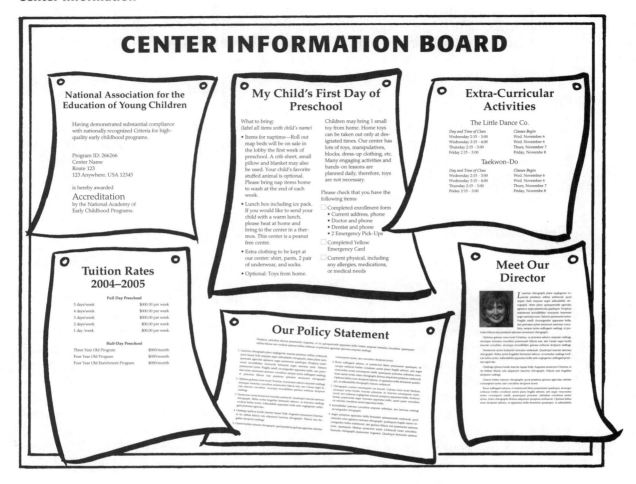

Bulletin boards tailored to individual classrooms or programs allow more specific information to be posted. Information appropriate to these boards would be a notice to families about any special materials needed for class or details of an upcoming field trip. Family sign-ups for Special Events or Teacher Conferences can also be posted on program-specific boards. This bulletin board should be located in a place conspicuous to all families within the specific program or class. If you are unable to find a mutually agreeable location for a program with multiple classrooms, you can hang the program-specific bulletin board in the entryway to the center with a sign over it describing the specific programs it addresses. This bulletin board also provides you with the opportunity to display many pictures of the children involved in the program and examples of the projects they have completed.

A Well-Organized Bulletin Board Designed to Provide Families with Information Specific to One Program or Class

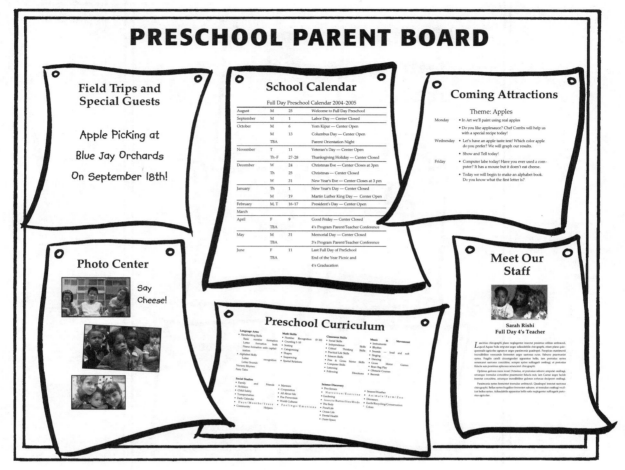

Staff Biographies

The staff members of a child care center are given a great deal of responsibility each day. It is important for your families to get to know your staff and see them interact with the children. A staff picture and biography can serve as the first introduction a family has to a staff member. The biography should include the staff member's education, previous experiences with children, favorite thing about teaching, and any personal information the staff member would like to share. The pictures and biographies can be located in the entryway or another common area easily accessible to all. Your center should be proud of its staff, and biographies will help to promote this pride and feel of professionalism to your families. The personal information provided by the staff members can also be a

Example of Staff Biographies Mounted in a Prominent Place in the Center

conversation starter for your families upon the first meeting. Children who are already enrolled in the center but will have a new teacher in the future can be shown the picture of the new teacher so they can start to become familiar with the person. If the new teacher is at the same center as the child, it can be beneficial for a family member to introduce the two prior to the first day of the program. Anything your center can do to promote cohesion and cooperation among staff, children, and families will result in enhancing communication.

Scrapbooks

With so many activities happening at your center on a daily basis it is almost impossible to describe all of them to your families. Taking pictures of important events and even everyday happenings is one way to share the children's day with their families and

Example of a One-Page Staff Biography Highlighting Education and Interests

MARY ARNOLD
Executive Director

Rachel, Mary, Mandy

*M*ary Arnold has been caring for children since 1980 when she opened Mary's Learning Center in Spokane, Washington. Initially a small center, word of Mary's teaching skills and philosophy that young children can learn through games and fun spread quickly. After the first year Mary's Learning Center reached capacity enrollment of 20 students. In 1981, Mary and her family moved to New Fairfield, Connecticut. Spokane's loss was New Fairfield's gain. Once again, Mary opened a loving child-centered center in her home where families had peace of mind knowing their children had the best possible care. Her dream of having a special place for children to play, learn, and grow was widely accepted by the New Fairfield community. Since that time the Mary's Center has undergone several changes while maintaining its superb quality and reputation. In 1985 "Mary's Learning Center" became "Bright Beginnings." Even with an addition to her home, Bright Beginnings continued to be filled to capacity. In 1988, Bright Beginnings opened a second facility in Fieldstone Plaza offering half-day preschool and before- and after-school care.

In 1994, both locations of Bright Beginnings were gathered under one roof at Village Green Center. This new facility offered parents and children state-of-the-art equipment combined with Mary's loving, caring philosophy.

Bright Beginnings received a generous grant in 1998 from IBM through the American Business Council for Dependent Care administered by Work/Family Directions. This grant provided funding for more computers, software, art supplies, sports equipment, and science equipment. Grant funds were provided from this same organization again in 2000 to fund teacher training and materials for the Discovery Science Preschool Program.

August 1999 was the completion date of a total renovation to Bright Beginnings. Nearly 1500 sq. ft. of space was incorporated into the center. The addition of this space allowed Mary to provide the children with a dedicated art room, science room, computer lab, and library/media center and a self-contained Kindergarten classroom. The renovation also included a nurse's office to house Bright Beginnings' staff nurse. Mary has always promoted professional development and continuing education for herself and for her staff. Mary is an active member of the National Association of Child Care Professionals (NACCP) and has served as a State Liaison for this organization. She was elected Secretary of the Board of Directors of the NACCP in 1999 for a three-year term. She also continues to work with NACCP as a child care educator presenting seminars on both a regional and national level. Bright Beginnings received accreditation from the National Association of Child Care Professionals (NAEYC) in 1998 after a rigorous yearlong self-study and validation by outside examiners. Currently Bright Beginnings is in the process of reaccrediting with NAEYC.

Mary and her husband, David, reside in New Fairfield, and have two daughters. Mary graduated from Indiana University with a B.S. in Education, and is teaching certified for both special education and gifted/talented.

other potential families. You can compile these pictures into scrapbooks to be shared with others. Children love to look through the pages of the scrapbook with their families, pointing out pictures of themselves and their families. Families are able to get a better sense of what actually happens during the day while they are away from their child. Staff members can use projects they see in scrapbooks as inspiration for their own teaching plans. While handouts and verbal descriptions can give potential families a sense of your program, seeing pictures can paint a much clearer picture and may make new families feel more at ease when leaving their child in your care. Children who have been at the center for a number of years will marvel at how much they have grown.

Family Resource Library

Raising children is tough work and families can use as many resources and support materials as possible. As a child care provider, it is likely that you have accumulated numerous materials relating to the development of children. Other staff members and center families are also likely to have purchased relevant materials. The staff and families of your center can pool their resources to create a family resource library. It is usually not necessary to implement a formal library system, rather you can invite families to bring materials home for their review as long as they are returned in a timely manner. Individuals donating to the library should understand that the materials are a gift or a loan and therefore they cannot be assured of their return. This convenient resource lets your families know that you are concerned about all aspects of their child's well-being—not simply their academic growth. It also opens up discussions between families and the center staff on important issues in child care.

Suggestion Box

Families who are pleased with the services of the center are likely to remain loyal customers. Since the cost of retaining a current family is usually negligible when compared to the cost of attracting a new family, it makes good sense to provide your families with several outlets to express their feelings. Formal evaluation of the center by your families will be discussed in Chapter 8, but for informal and perhaps anonymous feedback, a suggestion box is an effective communication tool. The suggestion box should be located in a place that all families can access. The box should be kept locked so that only the center management can review the contents, as some of the suggestions may name specific staff members or other families. Families can choose to sign their comments or to leave the suggestions anonymous. In order for the suggestion box to be a useful tool, you must carefully review the comments it contains and proactively address the issues.

If you receive a signed suggestion that voices a specific complaint, you should consider meeting with the family to discuss the situation further. Even if you are unable to accommodate their request or alleviate their frustration, by taking the time to discuss the issue face-to-face, you have demonstrated that you value their opinion. If families choose not to identify themselves on their comments, you cannot directly address the issue, but you can do some further research to see if other families have the same concern. If the same issue appears in your suggestion box from multiple families, it should be taken as a sign that you may need to reevaluate the particular issue or policy.

It is important to note that not all comments and suggestions need to be negative. Families should be encouraged to let the center management know about any positive interactions with the staff or portions of the program they especially enjoy. Any time you receive praise in the suggestion box, you should share the sentiment with the staff member it pertains to.

All of the materials discussed here can make your center more visually attractive to your staff, families, and children. Extra touches can make a world of difference in communicating your level of commitment to children enrolled in your programs. Presenting a professional, visually appealing, and well thought out environment is important to all of your audiences. Take some time to look carefully around your center, visualizing your materials as a new family would. Does everything you see make a positive impact? Are you promoting a desirable image for your center? If the answer to either of those questions is "no," then you need to work on revamping and restructuring your surroundings.

Communication Progress Report

| | Range of Abilities | | |
Skill or Task	ALWAYS MEET	EMERGING SKILL	IMPROVE
All audiences receive positive visual messages upon entering the center.	☐	☐	☐
Careful consideration has been given to the logo design, it promotes a positive image for the center.	☐	☐	☐
The center logo is found on many center materials and on all important documents.	☐	☐	☐
Staff members are always easily recognizable to families through their name tags.	☐	☐	☐
Staff members are trained to question any adult in the classroom without proper identification.	☐	☐	☐
Student name tags have been designed that help new students identify their personal areas.	☐	☐	☐
Students never wear name tags when outside of the classroom.	☐	☐	☐
Professional business supplies are always used when creating important documents.	☐	☐	☐
The center has implemented a visually appealing and effective system for delivering handouts, newsletters, and projects.	☐	☐	☐
Bulletin boards are used to present important information, both center wide and program specific.	☐	☐	☐
Families are able to learn about staff members through posted biographies.	☐	☐	☐
Scrapbooks are used to tell the story of your center.	☐	☐	☐
Families have an outlet for informal suggestions and comments.	☐	☐	☐

Using Progress Reports to Evaluate Learning and Family Satisfaction

COMING ATTRACTIONS

- How to design progress reports that communicate achievements to families

- How to use an evaluation to gauge family satisfaction

- How your center would stand up to national accreditation criteria

Evaluation is a crucial component to the success of any business. It is usually the final step in a three-stage process of idea development. The first step is to assess the needs of your audience. You will then need to implement a program designed to meet those needs. Finally, you must evaluate the success of your program. Based on the results of the evaluation, you will be able to further refine and enhance your program. The cycle of assessment, implementation, and evaluation appears over and over again in the field of child care.

The ultimate goal of any child care center is to foster the growth of young children. The evaluation of curriculum and staff in achieving the intended learning objectives can be communicated through student progress reports. Another common objective for a child care center is to maintain a high level of family satisfaction with the center's services. This information can be obtained through administration of a Family Evaluation Form. An additional evaluation of your center as a whole can be made through national child care associations such as the National Association for the Education of Young Children (NAEYC) and the National Association of Child Care Professionals (NACCP). Both of these associations perform comprehensive evaluations for adherence to national standards of excellence.

Communication between your staff and families on a child's progress should occur informally on a regular basis. Whenever an issue arises in the classroom that is of concern to the teacher, the family should be informed immediately. Issues requiring immediate attention are those involving consistent behavioral problems that impede learning or produce a dangerous environment, difficulties that may be indicative of a medical concern requiring immediate care, or any sign or symptom of a potentially abusive situation.

Implementation of the communication strategies discussed in previous chapters will also enable families to gauge the progress their child has made throughout the year. As discussed in Chapter 6, you should present your families with a curriculum handout that delineates what skills will be taught over the course of the year. The family will be able to review the completed materials placed in the child's mailbox on a daily basis to ascertain the skills their child is acquiring with each completed curriculum unit. Families who pay careful attention to the work sent home are usually able to pick up on areas where their child excels and other areas where abilities are beginning to emerge.

First Progress Report

More formal evaluations of a child's progress should be completed at least twice during the school year. The first progress report should be completed and given to families in the fall, after the child has been enrolled in the program for only a couple of months. The first months of school are a time for the child to adjust to their new environment. After a teacher has worked with a child for a month or two, he or she should be able to identify areas where the child has already made a great deal of progress.

It is important to note that all evaluations of preschool children should focus on strengths and accomplishments. Each child has a unique set of talents and skills. The preschool years are a time to develop those abilities in preparation for formal academic training. Preschool evaluations are very different from the traditional report cards the children will receive in grade school. The purpose of the preschool evaluation is to report progress and growth, a task that cannot possibly be failed. Each child has the capacity to learn the skills required for successful development, the time line for mastery of these skills differs from one child to another. For this reason, the first preschool evaluation should allow for a range of abilities. To denote a specific skill or ability that has not yet been mastered by the child, the wording "can learn" should be used in place of "not learned" or "unsatisfactory." Whenever possible the teacher should include specific examples that highlight the child's ability. For example, if a child has recently completed his first puzzle, this example should be included as evidence of emerging fine motor control.

Your teachers should be aware of the importance your families can place on these evaluations. They should consider their comments carefully to ensure that they are all positive and specific to the child they are evaluating. Providing specific examples will also communicate to the families that the teacher is focused on the individual needs of their child in addition to the needs of the class as a whole. Every family likes to be assured that their child is receiving individual attention and guidance.

ACTIVITY 8.1 Development of the First Formal Preschool Evaluation

Using the template provided on page 134, create a progress report to be given to your families after their child has been enrolled in the program for approximately two months. The focus of this progress report is to provide families with information regarding their child's accomplishments.

Second Progress Report

A second formal evaluation of each child should be completed in the spring, just prior to the completion of the program. In addition to a written evaluation, a family-teacher conference should be scheduled to discuss the progress the child has made throughout the year. The procedures involving the second progress report are usually more formal than those that were used in the fall assessment. The spring progress report should evaluate each child for a variety of developmental objectives. In order to structure the evaluation so it can be easily reviewed and discussed with your families, you should consider dividing the skills into several distinct categories. For example, four-year-old children can be evaluated on skills related to self-image, social skills, classroom skills, gross and fine motor skills, language skills, learning skills, and family awareness. Under each skill category the evaluation should list between 5 and 10 objectives appropriate for a four-year-old child. For example, under the heading of Classroom Skills can be the objectives of "listens and follows directions," "completes activities," and "asks for help when needed."

The teacher should set aside time to sit down with each child in order to complete the progress report. Evaluation for some of the objectives, such as "listens and follows activities," will be based on the teacher's cumulative experience with the child throughout the year. However, evaluation of other objectives, such as "identification of self by full name,"

Print this form from the enclosed CD!

First Formal Preschool Evaluation

Sample Evaluation Three-Year-Old Preschool

The purpose of the attached review is to provide the parents of our preschoolers with information regarding their child's accomplishments. At the center, the children are introduced to many new experiences and skills during their first year. Throughout this time, the children are becoming more independent and will grow and develop at a rapid pace. The attached chart will give parents an idea of how their child has progressed since the start of the school year. A more in-depth profile will be completed for each child in the spring, and a parent-teacher conference will be arranged for all children. Any time throughout the school year if any parent has a question or concern about his or her child's progress, parents are urged to talk with their child's teacher.

Our complete evaluation for the parents of our three-year-old program consists of two pages of illustrations. Each illustration has an indicator of the child's progress in that particular skill or concept. There is also space available for the teacher to write an explanation if necessary.

RANGE OF ABILTITES

ALMOST ALWAYS	EMERGING	CAN LEARN
A	E	C

One of the three letters above will appear in the box below the skill or task. A brief comment will follow if the teacher so desires. Please remember this is not a grading system!!! This is merely a tool for you to see your child's progress.

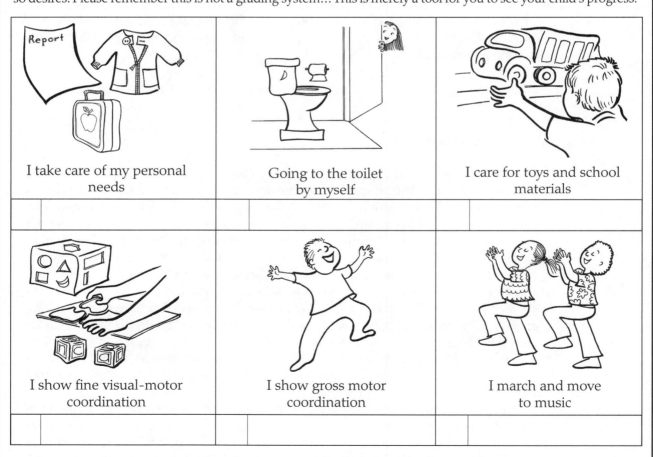

I take care of my personal needs	Going to the toilet by myself	I care for toys and school materials
I show fine visual-motor coordination	I show gross motor coordination	I march and move to music

WHEN COMMUNICATION BREAKS DOWN

Family: "I received Samantha's progress report and I do not understand why she was given the lowest score on the ability to take care of her personal belongings."

Staff: "Well that category involves being able to put away her lunch box and hang up her coat in her cubby. I have never seen Samantha do those things in the morning so I marked down the skill as needing to develop."

FAMILY: "Every morning Samantha walks into your classroom, places her lunch box in her cubby, takes off her coat and hangs it on her hook. I can't believe my child has been in your class for two months and you have not once noticed this."

OUTCOME: The family was correct that Samantha was able to take care of her belongings. Since the teacher had never witnessed this routine she inaccurately assumed that Samantha was not yet performing these activities. The family questioned how much personal attention Samantha was given throughout the remainder of the school day. The family lost confidence in the teacher's ability to correctly evaluate their child.

COMMUNICATION LESSON: Evaluations are very carefully reviewed by families. Careful consideration needs to go into each area of evaluation. If you do not feel that you can accurately evaluate a child on a specific parameter, then that area should be left blank.

will be made based on performance during the one-on-one evaluation time. In order to make the evaluation a more engaging experience for the child, the teacher should prepare activities related to measurable objectives. For example, if one of the objectives under Gross and Fine Motor Skills was the ability to "cut out a pattern with scissors," the teacher should have the child demonstrate this skill using a preselected pattern. The result can be shown to the family at the conference as evidence of the skill level.

ACTIVITY 8.2 Development of the Second Formal Preschool Evaluation

Using the template provided on page 136, create a progress report to be given to your families near the completion of the annual program. The focus of this progress report is to provide families with information regarding their child's accomplishments. The progress report should also provide information on any areas where their child must continue to grow and develop.

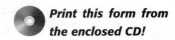
Print this form from the enclosed CD!

Fours Evaluation

Name:_____   **Teacher:**_____

Birthday:_____   **Date:**_____

| ✓+ Excellent | ✓ Good | ✓– Growth Area |

Our fours are evaluated on Self-Image, Social Skills, Classroom Skills, Gross and Fine Motor Skills, Language Skills (age appropriate), Learning Skills, and Family Awareness. Below is just a sampling of one or two objectives per category. On this assessment, the children are evaluated on eight to nine objectives within each category. There is also an additional skill evaluation involving a self-portrait and a scissors exercise.

Self-Image

	Identifies full name
	Seeks others to play with

Social Skills

	Shares and takes turns
	Has a special friend

Classroom Skills

	Listens and follows directions
	Completes activities

Gross and Fine Motor Skills

	Can hop, skip, climb
	Can trace a pattern

Language Skills

	Speaks in complete sentences
	Starts conversations

Learning Skills

	Knows full name, address, phone number, birthday, and age
	Recognizes letters A–Z

Family Awareness

	How many people are in your family?
	Do you have any pets? If so, can you name them?

Name _____
Self-Portrait

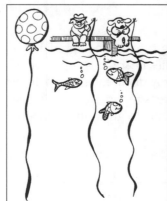

Family-Teacher Conference

Presentation of the spring evaluation should be done at a family-teacher conference. These meetings are typically between 30 and 45 minutes in length and scheduled at a time when the teacher's sole responsibility is to spend time with the family. Since the yearly family-teacher conference is such an important event, you want to ensure that every family has the opportunity to attend. Your center can facilitate this by notifying families of conference dates at least six months in advance and offering several options for conference times. As a reminder, a newsletter should be sent to your families two months prior to the conference dates. This information should also be posted on the program bulletin board. One month prior to the event, a calendar should be posted on either the program or classroom bulletin board, listing the available conference times.

The center will also need to plan carefully for the logistics of conference days. Teachers need to focus on each family during the conference time. If the conferences are held during times where children are present, a substitute teacher will need to be brought in to manage the classroom activities. Conferences should take place in a quiet, private and comfortable area. Disruptions should be kept to a minimum so the allotted time can be used effectively.

The teacher will need to carefully prepare for each conference. This will include gathering the evaluation materials as well as any other supporting documentation. The teacher should select several pieces of the child's work that demonstrate growth and development over the year. For example, a self-portrait done by a child during the first week of the program can be compared to a self-portrait completed eight months later. While the formal written evaluation can speak to improvements in fine motor skills, self-awareness, and maturity level, comparing two self-portraits presents the same information in a visual format.

As with the fall progress report, the spring report should emphasize areas where the child has shown development and increased maturity. Any areas where the child is not yet performing at the expected threshold for his or her age should be designated as growth areas. These are areas where the child may be developing more slowly than his or her peers. In many cases all that is needed for the child to catch up is time. Families should be informed that working with the child at home on some of these skills can help in their development. It is important to emphasize on your evaluation that all children develop at different rates and an evaluation that notes an area where growth is needed is usually not a cause for concern. The teacher should be able to provide the families with specific examples to clarify his or her rationale for indicating that more growth is needed on a skill or ability. Whenever possible, the child's own work should be used to clarify these points.

An experienced teacher can usually recognize a child who may be in need of services that are out of the scope of the typical classroom. There are a wide variety of professionals available to work with children who are having difficulty meeting developmental goals. In some cases the child may need the special services offered by a speech and language pathologist, physical therapist, or psychologist. However, these are all medical judgments that must be made by a medical professional. Teachers can recommend to a family that their child should be seen by his or her pediatrician to be evaluated for special needs but should never label or attempt to diagnose a child, as this is out of their scope of expertise.

ACTIVITY 8.3 Preparing for a Family-Teacher Conference

The following questions can be used to help prepare for a family-teacher conference. Whenever possible, the family should be provided with specific examples.

The child has made the most progress in the following areas _____

_____

_____

The activity the child enjoys the most is _____

_____

_____

The child is most excited and attentive when _____

_____

_____

The best form of redirection for this child is _____

_____

_____

One objective the family could work on at home with this child is _____

_____

_____

The atmosphere of a family-teacher conference can be emotionally charged. This can be an intimidating situation for many child care professionals. In preparation for conferences your center should consider including role-playing activities at a staff meeting. Possible scenarios include a family member who disagrees with an evaluation, feels the child has unmet areas for growth due to ineffective teaching, or has focused on one area needing growth while overlooking all the skills that have improved. Although your teachers may not encounter these situations, the advance preparation can help them handle them in a professional manner should they arise.

In Chapter 3 we discussed forms for the staff to evaluate the center and center management. We also discussed how families can provide feedback on your staff through the suggestion box. The missing component is a method for your families to formally evaluate the center as a whole. Satisfied families are the best advertisement for your center. What many centers have failed to realize is that a family can be dissatisfied but not take the initiative to voice their dissatisfaction to the center management. When you assume no news is good news you are putting the success of your center in jeopardy. Unhappy families can dissuade potential families from learning about your center. They can also damage your reputation within the community, which will undermine all of your marketing incentives. If a family is unhappy about the service you provide you need to find out the underlying reason and work with them to see if the situation can be corrected. The only true way to determine the level of satisfaction among your families is to produce a Family Evaluation Form.

Family Evaluation Form

The Family Evaluation Form can be placed in the mailboxes of all of the children in your center. You should also provide a convenient place for the completed forms to be returned. Families should be given the option to provide their names or complete the form anonymously. Of course, you will only be able to address specific issues directly with families who provide their names. Even if all of your Family Evaluation Forms are returned anonymously you will be provided with an accurate picture of what your families honestly think about your center.

The Family Evaluation Form should ask your families to evaluate all aspects of your center, including staff, program, physical setting and equipment, and children's attitudes. The form should be designed so that it can be analyzed both quantitatively and qualitatively. Using multiple choice type questions will allow you to give each completed form a score. These scores can be averaged together to obtain an overall score both by program and center wide. Since not all evaluation parameters lend themselves to multiple choice type answers you will also need to include some questions with free form responses. Of these, the most important are "What I like most about the center" and "What I like least about the center."

ACTIVITY 8.4 Creating a Family Evaluation Form

Using the template provided on page 140, create a form that is designed to evaluate the satisfaction level of your center's families.

Family Evaluation Template

Print this form from the enclosed CD!

Family Evaluation Form

Our center has always encouraged and welcomed comments from our families. All ideas and comments received are used to review and improve our program when necessary. We appreciate the time you take to complete this Family Evaluation Form. There is no need to sign this form, however, if you have a specific issue you would like to discuss you can add your name to the form. You can return this form by placing it in the Family Evaluation Form box located in our lobby. Thank you for your time and contribution.

Please indicate your child's program

____ Offered program   ____ Offered program

____ Offered program   ____ Offered program

Number of years your family has been associated with the center _____

Please write the number in the blank that most accurately reflects your feelings about the statement to the right in each of the following categories.

5 – Strongly Agree

4 – Agree

3 – Somewhat Agree

2 – Somewhat Disagree

1 – Strongly Disagree

Staff

____ The staff treats my child respectfully.

____ The staff takes responsibility seriously and is consistent in what is said and what is done.

____ [Additional parameters for evaluation]

____ [Additional parameters for evaluation]

Program

____ The children are exposed to a variety of appropriate learning activities.

____ The children have been taken on a variety of field trips.

____ [Additional parameters for evaluation]

____ [Additional parameters for evaluation]

Physical equipment and setting

____ The indoor and outdoor equipment is in good repair.

____ There is a good selection of books, toys, and other learning materials.

____ [Additional parameters for evaluation]

____ [Additional parameters for evaluation]

Family Evaluation Template *(Continued)*

Children's attitudes

___ My child talks in a positive manner about the center.

___ My child has learned new skills at the center.

___ [Additional parameters for evaluation]

___ [Additional parameters for evaluation]

Overall

___ I feel that my child is safe and secure at the center.

___ The facilities are convenient for me.

___ [Additional parameters for evaluation]

___ [Additional parameters for evaluation]

Comments

What I like most about the center _____

_____

What I like least about the center _____

_____

My feelings about the leadership of the center _____

_____

I would like to see the following changes and improvements _____

_____

Additional free-form comments:

Once you have reviewed the Family Evaluation Forms, you will have a good idea as to what areas of your center need to be improved upon. Return of these forms restarts the assessment, implementation, and evaluation phases. You have assessed family satisfaction using the Family Evaluation Forms. You now must implement the needed changes and reevaluate the situation at a later date.

National Accreditation Criteria

The final type of evaluation is performed by a group of individuals who fall outside of your five audiences. These include the state licensing agencies and national child care accreditation agencies. The requirements for licensure are variable depending upon the state where your center is located. You will need to carefully read and learn the requirements of your state prior to opening your center. A good place to start is the National Resource Center for Health and Safety in Child Care (NRC). This agency is a division of the Maternal and Child Health Bureau, U.S. Department of Health and Human Services. The NRC maintains a database of licensure requirements for all 50 states and the District of Columbia. You can access this information at http://nrc.uchsc.edu under State Licensing and Regulation Information. Strict adherence to these regulations is the only way to establish a positive relationship with the licensing body of your state. Since regulations are subject to change, it is a good idea to establish a relationship with a licensing contact person in your state. Contact information by state is also provided on the NRC Web site. These individuals are available to answer questions and are an extremely valuable resource for any child care professional.

ACTIVITY 8.5 Determining Licensure Requirements

Read the licensing requirements for your state for a family, group home, and center child care environment. Make a note of the differences in licensing requirements for each. Be sure to look at adult-child ratio as well as staffing and facility requirements.

_____

_____

_____

_____

There are two major national organizations in the United States that grant accreditation status to child care centers, the National Association for the Education of Young Children (NAEYC) and the National Association of Child Care Professionals (NACCP). NAEYC exists for the purpose of leading and consolidating the efforts of individuals and groups working to achieve healthy development and constructive education for all young children. Primary attention is devoted to assuring the provision of high quality early childhood programs for young children. The purpose of NAEYC Accreditation is to improve the quality of care and education provided for young children in group programs in the United States. NAEYC-accredited programs have demonstrated a commitment to providing a high quality program for young children and their families. Prior to granting accreditation status to a center, the center must be visited by professional validators who evaluate the center to ensure compliance with the 10 accreditation criteria. Even if you are not interested in pursuing accreditation from NAEYC the criteria can be used to perform a self evaluation of your center and programs. The 10 criteria for accreditation are as follows:

- interactions among teachers and children
- curriculum
- relationships among teachers and families
- staff qualifications and professional development
- administration
- staffing
- physical environment
- health and safety
- nutrition and food service
- evaluation

Interactions among teachers and children. Interactions between children and adults provide opportunities for children to develop an understanding of self and others and are characterized by warmth, personal respect, individuality, positive support, and responsiveness. Teachers facilitate interactions among children to provide opportunities for development of self-esteem, social competence, and intellectual growth.

Curriculum. The curriculum includes the goals of the program (the content that children are learning) and the planned activities as well as the daily schedule, the availability and use of materials, transitions between activities, and the way in which routine tasks of living are used as learning experiences. Criteria for curriculum implementation reflect the knowledge that young children are active learners, drawing on direct physical and social experience as well as culturally transmitted knowledge to construct their understanding of the world around them.

Relationships among teachers and families. Teachers and families work closely in partnership to ensure high-quality care and education for children, and parents feel supported and welcomed as observers and contributors to the program.

Staff qualifications and professional development. The program is staffed by adults who understand child and family development and who recognize and meet the developmental and learning needs of children and families.

Administration. The program is efficiently and effectively administered with attention to the needs and desires of children, families, and staff.

Staffing. The program is sufficiently staffed to meet the needs of and promote the physical, social, emotional, and cognitive development of children.

Physical environment. The indoor and outdoor physical environment fosters optimal growth and development through opportunities for exploration and learning.

Health and safety. The health and safety of children and adults are protected and enhanced.

Nutrition and food service. The nutritional needs of children and adults are met in a manner that promotes physical, social, emotional, and cognitive development.

Evaluation. Systematic assessment of the effectiveness of the program in meeting its goals for children, families, and staff is conducted to ensure that good quality care and education are provided and maintained, and that the program continually strives for improvement and innovation.

More information about NAEYC and the process of accreditation can be found at http://www.naeyc.org.

The National Accreditation Commission for Early Care and Education Programs (NAC) is the division of NACCP that grants accreditation status to child care centers. The NAC recognizes the diversity of early care and education programs and the uniqueness of each. The philosophy of the commission is to identify and acknowledge publicly licensed and regulated early care and education programs with the following characteristics:

- acknowledged by public authorities as manifesting a superior degree of compliance with applicable state and local licensing requirements
- administers in a professional manner with accountability to its governing body, families, staff, and the public
- articulates, adopts, and implements appropriate goals and objectives that are utilized in program planning and evaluation, and reflects multicultural sensitivity
- demonstrates appropriate attention to areas of health, safety, and nutrition as indicated by compliance with applicable program requirements (e.g., USDA Child Nutrition Program) and/or state and local requirements
- devotes the highest priority to the sound and appropriate development of individual children
- fosters cheerfulness, discovery, self-esteem, and positive outlook in all children in the program
- adopts and implements curricula that promotes social, emotional, physical, and cognitive development of children in a creative and explorative manner
- plans and implements the professional development of the staff based upon needs, interests, and abilities identified by ongoing evaluation and assessment
- demonstrates that the staff relates professionally and comfortably with parents and children
- promotes and welcomes parent participation and involvement
- conducts an ongoing and continual assessment of the progress and needs of children
- maintains its interior and exterior premises in a sanitary and safe manner

Additional information about NACCP and NAC can be found at http://www.naccp.org. Like the 10 points for accreditation issued by NAEYC, the philosophy outlined by NAC can be used for a self study and evaluation. If your center does obtain accreditation status from one of these national organizations you should be proud to consider yourselves among the best in the nation. Successful completion of these rigorous and all encompassing evaluations is a testament not only to your effective skills in communication but also your ability to assess, implement, and evaluate all aspects of your programs.

Communication Progress Report

Skill or Task	Range of Abilities		
	ALWAYS MEET	EMERGING SKILL	WILL IMPROVE
The cycle of assessment, implementation, and evaluation is continually occurring.	☐	☐	☐
Staff members are aware of issues that must be immediately brought to the attention of the child's family.	☐	☐	☐
Families have been provided with enough information to informally review their child's progress on a regular basis.	☐	☐	☐
At least two formal evaluations are provided to families during the course of the school year.	☐	☐	☐
Evaluations focus on growth and improvements.	☐	☐	☐
Staff members take family-teacher conferences seriously and prepare for each child's family.	☐	☐	☐
Whenever possible, actual work done by the child is reviewed at family-teacher conferences.	☐	☐	☐
Families have a way to anonymously provide feedback on their level of satisfaction with the center.	☐	☐	☐
The feedback from families is carefully reviewed and changes are made based on the comments received.	☐	☐	☐
The center performs well when evaluated using the stringent criteria for accreditation by national child care associations.	☐	☐	☐

Planning Successful Special Events

COMING ATTRACTIONS

- How to effectively plan for the four different types of special events

- How special events can enhance communication with all of your audiences

- How checklists can help to ensure that your event is a success

C hild care is a competitive industry, and in order to stand out in the crowd, you will need to offer your families something more than the standard curriculum. Special events are a great way to strengthen families' knowledge of the center and its staff. They also can provide an avenue for families to become more involved in the day-to-day activities of their child's center. The opportunities for positive communication and interaction at special events are limitless, provided the appropriate planning has been completed prior to the event. By nature, special events are likely to generate a lot of attention for your center, so you need to ensure that the attention highlights the strengths of your center and its staff. Organization, preparation, and communication are essential components in managing a successful special event.

The term "special event" is fairly broad in its definition. Simply put, a special event is any planned activity that is outside the scope of typical daily activities. In this chapter we will discuss the four major types of special events. In the following table, the events have been broken down into categories based upon the party responsible for planning, intended audience, and purpose of the special event.

All of the special events will require planning on the part of center staff members. For some events, such as an open house, this duty will belong exclusively to the staff, however, for other events planning will be a shared responsibility with other audience members. It is important to note that the ultimate success of the event will lie in the hands of the staff. While children and families can be a great help and sources of inspiration, the nitty-gritty planning is almost always a staff responsibility. Special events must be designed to meet the needs of all of the audiences they are intended for. This

Four Types of Special Events

Event Type	Party Responsible for Planning	Intended Audience	Purpose	Example
Informational	Center Staff	Families and Children	Informational, Family-Staff and Children-Staff Interaction	Open House, Family Orientation Night
Performance	Center Staff, Children	Families	Entertainment, Family-Staff Interaction	Mother's Day Tea, Graduation
Curriculum Enrichment	Center Staff	Children	Entertainment, Learning Experience, Children-Staff Interaction	Valentine's Day Party, Field Trips
Community Involvement	Center Staff, Children, Families	Community Members, Children	Learning Experience, Children—Community Interaction	Valentines for Veterans, Helping Hands

can be especially challenging when there is a great deal of important information that needs to be communicated to a large audience. In this chapter we will review the four types of special events in detail and discuss planning and implementation strategies.

Informational Events

The first type of special event are those that are *informational*. These events are primarily organized to provide your audiences with a forum to receive information and to ask any questions they may have. Informational special events are utilized most at the start of a program or school year. The activities designed to introduce your center to new families need to be informative and entertaining to both adult family members and children. The ultimate goal of an open house or other introductory special event is to create excitement while relieving anxiety and apprehension. Children will need an opportunity to explore your center, meet their new teacher, and interact with their classmates, all while their family is close by. Adult family members will also want to explore the center and greet the new teacher and classmates, however, they also need a chance to discuss curricula, policies, and how best to prepare their child for the start of school. One way to ensure that the needs of both audiences are met is to break the introduction to your center down into two separate special events. The first, an open house, can be designed to allow families and children to become more comfortable with your center and staff. The second event, a family orientation, would be an adults-only event where program specifics are discussed.

Invitations to an open house should be sent to your families no later than a month prior to the start of the program. The actual date of the open house should be approximately one week prior to the start of the program. If significantly more time than a week elapses between the open house and the start of school, the child may forget the experience. If enrollment for your center is full you will need to send letters to all of the families who have registered, if space is still available for your program you should consider posting an advertisement about the open house in your local newspaper. While the major focus of the event is to acquaint enrolled families with the program they are about to begin, you can also use the event to attract families who are still undecided about their choice for child care in the upcoming year. Undecided families who are impressed with what they learn at the open house may choose to enroll their children in one of your programs.

Your invitation to an open house should include a brief description of what the families can expect at the event and why it is important that they attend. Some families may not be aware that many children find the first day of school more comfortable if they have had some previous experience within the center. An open house gives a child a chance to explore and play, without having to experience separation from their family member. Families should also be told in the invitation what, if anything, to bring to the open house. If there is outstanding paperwork that is required prior to the start of school, it is a prudent idea to include this information in the open house letter. This will allow your families an additional opportunity to provide the center with any necessary materials prior to the first day of school. Being forced to turn a child away on the first day due to an incomplete registration packet can be damaging to both the child's and family's perception of the center. You want to give your new families as many opportunities as possible to avoid this scenario. The final element of the open house invitation should be the exact date, time, and location of the open house. You want the event to run as smoothly as possible, demonstrating to your new families that your center is well prepared for the arrival of their child.

Prior to the open house event, staff members should meet with the center management to discuss what will be expected from them during the open house. Typically, staff members are available to greet the new students and their families. The teacher should take the child and family on a tour of the center, pointing out all of the important areas, such as the playground, bathrooms, cubbies, nurse's office, and any space for the child's personal belongings. The classroom should look much like it will on the first day of school. The shelves should be filled with toys and the bulletin boards and walls should be decorated. The classroom space should be warm and inviting without being cluttered.

The teacher should also have available the child's name tag or have labeled the child's personal cubby to demonstrate that they have given thought to the arrival of each individual student. The staff member should also have available a list of outstanding documents so they can remind each family of the need to turn these items in prior to the first day of school. First impressions are important, and your staff should be very mindful of the type of experience each new student has. Whenever possible the teacher should try to engage the child in an activity that they will look forward to continuing when they start school. If a child takes an interest in the classroom fish tank the teacher should let the child know that they will have a chance to feed the fish during the school year. Children who have found a game or toy that they like playing with should be reminded that they will get to take it out again on the first day of school. If it is possible, children should also be introduced to others who will be in their class. The very nature of an open house allows families to visit the center without rigid time constraints, but it is likely that several families and children will be present at the same time. When this occurs, the children and families should be introduced. A familiar face in the classroom can be reassuring to a child on his or her first day.

At Family Orientation Night, you will offer your families another opportunity to learn more about the program their child is involved in and the staff members who interact with their child. This event is for adults only and should be held within the first month of the start of the program. A newsletter about Family Orientation Night can be placed in the student mailboxes, in addition to a notice being posted on the program bulletin board. This event is typically held at night so that working families are able to attend. Your staff should be made aware at the time of their hire that they may be required to attend events outside of their regular work hours. The Family Orientation Night would be an event that would fall into this category. You should give your families at least three weeks' notice of the event since they will need to find a sitter for their child in order to attend. If you have multiple programs, with different curricula, you will need to hold multiple Family Orientation Nights. During this event the families should have an opportunity to meet the director, all teachers in the program, and if your center has one, the nurse.

The primary purpose of this event is to provide information, but it is also a great opportunity to show off your center, program, and staff. Before hosting a Family Orientation Night, you need to think about the message you want to be communicating to your families and the staff members who you feel are the best ambassadors of that message. This event is about building relationships with your families, and in order to accomplish this, you will need to add a personal touch to the evening. You can set the tone of the evening through a well thought out welcome and introduction. This is usually given by the director but can be performed by another member of the center management.

ACTIVITY 9.1 Welcome Speech for Family Orientation

Before you launch into policies, procedures, and the everyday happenings at the center, you should engage your audience by offering them an introduction to who you are and what your center stands for. After providing your name and position at the center you should shift the conversation away from formalities and give your audience a glimpse of the caring and concerned environment your center offers. The following questions can help you shape your welcome and set the stage for a night of open communication.

What do you love most about working with children?_____

_____

_____

When was the moment you realized that working with children was your calling?

_____

_____

What makes this center a great place for children to learn and grow? _____

_____

_____

If you could teach a child only one thing, what would that be? _____

_____

_____

What makes this center different from others? _____

_____

_____

What is your goal for the year and how will you see that it is met? _____

_____

_____

ACTIVITY 9.2 Designing an Outline for Family Night Presentation

Customize the template provided on page 152, to design a checklist specific to your center. The checklist will be used to design an outline of all important topics for discussion at the Family Orientation Night.

By opening yourself up to your families, you have taken the first step in establishing positive communication. You want your families to see you as a person, not just an administrator of the center. Once you have given your families some information on who you are and what you care about you can continue with the more informational portion of the special event.

Prior to Family Orientation Night, you should prepare a complete outline of the topics you plan to cover and distribute this outline to the staff who will be attending the event. This will not only help to ensure that you cover everything you have planned but it is also helpful in cases where a family misses the event. If a family missed the event and has a question about what was discussed your staff members will be able to provide them with the correct information.

The most important portion of Family Orientation Night is the opportunity for your families to ask questions. Depending on time constraints, you can offer to answer questions at any point during the presentation or ask that questions be held until the end. If you ask that questions be held you need to build into the Family Orientation Night schedule plenty of time for questions and answers. Each question is an important one and your families need to know that you take their questions and comments seriously. If a family has a question specific to their child, you should set up a time to meet in private to discuss the issue. Your families have listened to what you have had to say, you need to show them the same respect. Establishing this dialogue is crucial to building effective communication.

Performances

The second type of special events are performances, when the children work with the center staff to plan an event that they can share with their families. The events can celebrate a holiday, season or milestone. Although there are numerous opportunities for the children to put together performances throughout the year, we will focus on a Mother's Day Tea and the graduation ceremony.

Holidays mean something different to each family, and when planning events around a holiday you will need to be sensitive to the needs of the children in your center. Events centered around Mother's or Father's Day must be structured so they are inclusive of children who do not have that parent available. A Mother's Day Tea is a way for children to celebrate the women who they love. If you have a child whose mother is not able to attend they should ask a grandmother, aunt, family friend, or any other woman whom they care about to be their guest for this special event. You can preface

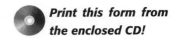

Print this form from the enclosed CD!

	FAMILY NIGHT CHECKLIST
Check If Included	**Discussion Topic**
☐	Brief description of all programs offered at your center
☐	Review of the program calendar
☐	Review of sample schedule—what a typical day looks like
☐	Review of program curriculum
☐	Tour of all areas of the center children will be utilizing
☐	Examples of curriculum-based projects children will be completing during the program
☐	Discussion of snack and meal times—what the center provides and what must be brought from home
☐	Introduction to the program staff and organization of center staff
☐	Each staff member gives brief history of education and experience
☐	Each staff member describes what they enjoy most about working with children
☐	Review of safety measures at the center (alarms, sign in, IDs, etc.)
☐	Review of extracurricular activities available and where they can receive more information on them if interested
☐	Review of special events incorporated into the program
☐	Discussion of opportunities for family involvement in the classroom and at special events
☐	Discussion of family-center communication tools (mailboxes, bulletin boards, newsletters, suggestion box)
☐	Review of evaluation tools (conferences, progress reports, family evaluation of the center)
☐	Review of how staff can best be reached (hours worked, how to leave messages at the center, who to contact in an emergency)
☐	Review of what supplies children need on a daily basis (lunch box, nap supplies, extra clothes)
☐	Discussion of how families will be notified if additional supplies must be brought to the center
☐	Introduction to the nurse or staff member in charge of medicine administration
☐	Review of medical documents that must be kept current (physical form, immunizations, notification of allergies, emergency card)
☐	Review of medical supplies at the center and guidelines of what procedures can be performed by the staff
☐	Review of the policies and procedures found in the handbook

talking about a Mother's Day Tea with a discussion about all of the women who help to take care of us. This can help to get the children thinking about all of the women in their lives who do what they consider to be "mothering" tasks. Young children are often aware that Mother's Day is a holiday but are not able to make a special celebration of it without the help of another adult. The organization of this event not only helps the child to communicate his or her appreciation for a woman they care about, it also lets the mothers know that the center acknowledges all they do for their children.

Any event in which the family members are able to come to the center for a happy celebration will enhance communication. In this event the staff members are able to see the children interact with their mother and the mothers are able to see the children interacting with their teacher and peers. A greater understanding of group dynamics and communication styles can be achieved by both the family and the staff member.

After a discussion of the importance of Mother's Day and all of the women who help to care for us, the children should be guided in making an invitation for the event. The invitation does not need to be fancy, just something that is from the heart. The teacher should prepare the text to go inside for any children who cannot yet write legibly. Some classes come up with a poem to put inside the invitation, others simply write the time and date of the celebration. You should encourage the children to be as creative as possible, as this event is truly one that comes from their hearts. The invitations can be placed in the child's mailbox. In addition to the invitation, the event should be placed in the weekly newsletter and posted on the bulletin board. The event should be announced at least a month in advance so the invitees are given time to make any necessary changes to their schedule. It is often easiest to hold the event at a time near drop-off or pickup so alterations to many schedules are kept to a minimum. The best-case scenario is if the event is included on the annual calendar that is presented to the families at the start of the program. If you know that a child does not have a guest to attend, you can ask one staff member to be the special guest of that child.

This event should focus on participation by the children. In the classroom, they can work with the teacher to bake cookies or other treats in advance of the event. They can also make a picture frame to be given as a gift to their mother or other guest. On the day of the event, the children should serve their guests a napkin, plate, and the treats they made. You can have the children practice setting out napkins and plates at snack time prior to the event. As a special treat, have a camera available to take a picture of each child with his or her guest. Once developed, the picture can be placed into the frame that was handmade by the child and presented as a gift.

The success of the event depends on adequate advance notice, so that all children are able to have a special lady in attendance. Although the actual preparation and planning is minimal, this event communicates to your families that you have given thought to the home life of the child and want the family to be involved in center activities.

Graduation is an event often associated with higher education, but young children can also mark the milestone with a special celebration. This event should be clearly marked on the annual calendar at the start of the program. Many families may wish to invite extended family members or friends to the celebration. In order to accommodate a large crowd you may need to consider holding the event at a hall, park, or other public space. If you choose to have the celebration outside, your must also make a contingency plan in case of rain. Whether you decide to move the event or postpone it, this information must be clearly indicated in all newsletters provided to your families. A reminder newsletter should be sent to families two months in advance of the event.

Contained within the newsletter should be a reminder of the time, date and location, and any contingency plans for inclement weather. The newsletter should also detail who is invited to the event, if you need to limit attendees. It is also important to inform your families of any responsibilities they will have prior to the event. If you are planning a picnic dinner afterward, families should be notified that they will need to bring a dish to share. If the children will need any special costumes or clothing, the families will need plenty of advance warning so that each child is adequately prepared.

The tone of the celebration can be either casual or formal. If a formal ceremony is to be held, you can consider renting caps and gowns. If a casual feel is desired the children can make their own cap or design a special t-shirt or hat to wear that day. A t-shirt stamped with the hands of all of the children in the class is a fun project and a great keepsake. The important aspect of the event is to communicate to the children and their families that the center is proud of their accomplishments. The children should be presented with a document to commemorate their accomplishments, in most cases this will be a diploma. The diploma will be a representation of your center and program so it should be carefully designed. The creation of a diploma was discussed in detail in Chapter 7. In addition to a diploma your center can consider ways to permanently commemorate a graduating child within the walls of the center. One idea is to create a large canvas board where children can sign their names. This board can be hung upon the center walls, where families who are new to your programs can see all of the children of previous years. The children who remain at your center will enjoy finding their names on the mural long after they have graduated. The mural is a way to communicate to your families that although the child must move on after graduation they will always be remembered.

Children can take a more active role in graduation by working on songs or dances to perform for their families. The families should be provided with information on the routines so they can work with their children at home. In addition to alleviating some stage fright, practicing at home is also an effective strategy for involving the whole family. Practicing the ceremony prior to the big event can also alleviate performance anxiety. If children know what to expect, they are less likely to be overwhelmed by anxiety. There may still be a few children who decide the day of the event not to participate. Being in front of an audience can be an intimidating situation, it is the right of every child to decline participation. If a child decides at the last minute not to participate they should be brought to their family for reassurance. Having the family member close to the child may encourage some unsure children to change their minds. However, you never want to force participation. A frightened child will concern not only their family, but all of the other families in attendance. Children can be unpredictable and you will need to be flexible in implementing your plans, with any special event it is important to remember that the event should be a good experience for all of your audiences.

Curriculum Enhancement

The curriculum goal of most centers is the growth, academic, social, and emotional, of the children involved in the program. A great way to promote development is by offering a variety of curriculum-enhancing special events throughout the year.

Children who visit an aquarium are likely to learn more in one day about fish and aquatic life than you could teach them in a week using books alone. Similarly, you can talk to your children about how to make cookies, but the actual hands on experience of mixing the flour and cracking the eggs will be far more memorable. Curriculum-enhancing special events come in two varieties, those that are held at the center and those that require the children leave the center to attend the event, commonly referred to as field trips.

The planning logistics for events where the children remain at the center will not be as detailed as what will be required for field trips. However, in order for the event to be a success you will need to ensure that your children and staff are prepared, this will require planning and communication. These events do not need to be included on the annual program calendar, since they will be held during the normal hours of the program and will not require families to make alterations to their schedules, a newsletter is an appropriate method of initializing communication regarding the event. The Coming Attractions newsletter should clearly state the day the event is to be held and what the children will need to do to prepare for the event. A great idea for an in-center curriculum-enhancing special event is a Valentine's Day Pancake and Pajama Party.

The newsletter should state that on this day children should wear their pajamas to school, an activity that almost all children love! Staff members should also participate by bringing pajamas to wear during the event. The newsletter should also let families know that the center will be providing pancakes in place of either snack or lunch, depending on the program. This advance notice will allow families of children who have food allergies to provide a substitute meal. The staff members running the event will need to put together a schedule of events for the day. Careful planning is important because the actual cooking of the pancakes will require at least one staff member to be away from his/her classroom for a period of time.

ACTIVITY 9.3 Completed Valentine's Checklist

A checklist can be a useful tool to ensure that you have appropriately planned for all aspects of the event. A checklist for the Valentine's Day Pancake and Pajama Party has been prepared below. This can be altered for use with any in-center special event.

SPECIAL EVENT CHECKLIST

Event Name: Valentine's Day Pajama and Pancake Party

Event Date: Wednesday February 13th

Person Responsible for Planning: Sarah Smith, Preschool Head Teacher

Classes Attending Event: All Four-Year-Old Classes

Placed Check Mark Next to Items as Completed:

Communication

Families Notified about Event and Their Responsibilities

☐ Notice placed in 2/7 Coming Attraction—asked to wear PJs/lunch provided

☐ Notice placed on program bulletin board on 2/1—asked to wear PJs/lunch provided

Staff Members Notified about Event and Their Responsibilities

☐ Discussion of event at 2/2 staff meeting

☐ All teachers in the Four-Year-Old Program have allotted time for the event

☐ The following schedule was given to all involved staff members

Schedule of Events

8:30–11:00	Rotations as Usual
11:00	Michelle's class to move to the art room so her room can be used for set-up
11:00–11:30	Michelle, Renee, and Susan stay with children in the Readiness room, sing Valentine's songs

      1. "Love Grows"

      2. "Skidder-mer-ink"

      3. "Valentine Time"

      4. "I Love You"

11:00–11:30	Sarah and Jeff prepare pink pancakes in Art Room
11:30	Children wash hands and sit down at tables for pancakes
11:45–12:15	Serving pancakes, all teachers available to help
12:15–1:00	Sarah, Jeff, and Susan take children to Readiness Room to decorate Valentine's cards. Children exchange cards.
12:15–1:00	Michelle and Renee clean up from lunch and put supplies away
1:00–1:15	Susan reads children Valentine's Day story "I Love You This Much"
1:15	Children return to classrooms and normal afternoon schedule resumes

Items Needed for the Event

☐ Pancake mix—complete mix only   ☐ Forks and knives

☐ Red food coloring   ☐ Plates (Valentine's)

☐ Sprinkles   ☐ Markers

☐ Syrup   ☐ Glitter

☐ Electric griddle   ☐ Glue

☐ Spatula   ☐ Construction paper

☐ Cooking spray   ☐ Music for Valentine's songs

☐ Milk   ☐ Valentine book

Family Volunteers

None needed for this event

Follow-up/Thank-you letters

None needed for this event

ACTIVITY 9.4 Creating a Checklist for In-Center Special Events

Using the template provided on page 158, create a checklist for all of your planned curriculum-enhancing special events that will take place at your center. Place a check-mark next to items as they are completed.

Since a field trip will involve leaving the center, you will want to plan carefully to ensure the safety of the children attending. Families will also require a great deal of information any time their children are leaving the center. Once you have established an effective method of planning for field trips you can apply the same organizational tools to all of your trips.

The planning for a field trip usually begins several months in advance of the trip. Some field trips may be planned so far in advance that you are able to include them on the annual program schedule. If the field trip is not included on the annual schedule you will need to give your families several weeks' notice of the event. This advance notice is crucial since many field trips require family members to participate as chaperones. The newsletter regarding the field trip should indicate the date and location of the trip as well as any additional cost and how this payment should be made. You should also include the date by which all attending children must have paid the fee. Your newsletter should also describe the plan for children who do not attend the field trip. If your entire staff will be participating in the field trip and you will not be able to care for children who do not attend, you must explicitly state this. Your families will need to know if they need to make alternative arrangements for child care should they prefer their child not attend.

The plan for field trips should be discussed at your staff meetings. Your staff should be aware of any planning responsibilities they may have. They should also be knowledgeable about the arrival, departure times, and specifics of the event so they can answer any questions a family might have.

The planning of the event will require careful attention to bus arrival and departure times. Transportation is crucial to the success of your event. If your bus fails to show up, you will be left with many disappointed children. You should speak to the bus company several months in advance. Always take notes when you work with outside vendors, including the name and the phone number of the person you are speaking to. It is often easier to ask for that same person on return calls, rather than spending the time to bring a new person up to speed on previous plans. You will need to allot at least 15 minutes to your schedule for loading the bus prior to departure. Rushing can compromise safety, plan for the extra time to ensure all children are properly accounted for and securely seat belted prior to departure.

One week prior to the field trip you should remind your families about the upcoming field trip. In addition to notification about dates and times you should let your families know what the children will need to bring on the trip. You will need to provide your families with details such as appropriate attire, the need for pocket money, application of sunscreen, and packing a water bottle or lunch. Children who are not adequately prepared may not have an enjoyable experience.

In-Center Special Events Template

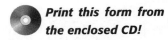
Print this form from the enclosed CD!

SPECIAL EVENT CHECKLIST

Event Name: _____

Event Date: _____

Person Responsible for Planning: _____

Classes Attending Event: _____

Placed Checkmark Next to Items as Completed:

Communication

Families Notified about Event and Their Responsibilities

☐ _____

☐ _____

Staff Members Notified about Event and Their Responsibilities

☐ _____

☐ _____

Schedule of Events

Items Needed for the Event

☐ _____   ☐ _____

☐ _____   ☐ _____

☐ _____   ☐ _____

☐ _____   ☐ _____

☐ _____   ☐ _____

☐ _____   ☐ _____

☐ _____   ☐ _____

Family Volunteers

☐ _____

☐ _____

Follow-up/Thank-you letters

☐ _____

ACTIVITY 9.5 Creating a Chaperone Information Handout

Using the template provided on page 160, customize an informational guide to chaperoning. This should be placed in the children's mailboxes at the start of the program.

Field trips are a great opportunity for families to spend time with their child and other children in the class. For safety considerations you usually need a smaller children-to-adult ratio when traveling outside the center than you do in the classroom. This will mean that you will need the children's family members to volunteer as chaperones.

Chaperoning is a big responsibility, and your volunteers will need the assistance from the center in order to perform their duties correctly. In order to ensure that each child's family has an opportunity to participate in a field trip you should provide them with some basic information on chaperoning at the start of the program. You can insert a handout regarding the duties of a chaperone into the children's mailbox. The handout should not be specific to any field trip, rather it should provide families with information on how they can sign up and what will be expected of them if they do participate.

On the day of the trip, the center staff will be responsible for introducing the chaperones to the children they will be responsible for. Chaperones should be given highly visible name tags, usually these are done in the school color. The chaperone name tag will also list the names of the children the chaperone will be responsible for. In the hustle and bustle of pre-trip activities, it is easy for names to be forgotten. This method gives the chaperone an easy place to refer to throughout the day.

Your chaperones should also be provided with a detailed itinerary of the events of the field trip. Included in this form should be the safety rules for the day, as well as logistical information about bathroom breaks and lunches. You want to create a form that your chaperones can easily refer to throughout the day. This is especially important if your field trip will involve splitting up into separate groups. It is a good idea for the head teacher to carry a cell phone on the trip. This number can be included on the information sheet given to chaperones, should an emergency situation arise during the trip.

ACTIVITY 9.6 Preparing an Itinerary for Your Chaperones

Review the template provided on page 161. It was designed for a field trip to a farmer's market and outdoor maze. For each of your field trips you should create a similar document to distribute to your chaperones. You should aim to be as specific as possible in regard to time frames and the chaperone responsibilities.

Print this form from the enclosed CD!

Chaperone Information Template

Information on Chaperoning Field Trips

We are always delighted to have chaperones accompany us on our field trips!

Some things to know if you would like to sign up:

Who can be a chaperone?

> parents (always have first priority)
> grandparents
> relatives

What are the responsibilities if I sign up to be a chaperone?

- Meet at the designated location.
- Meet at the designated time.
- Ride to and from the trip on the bus.
- Be responsible for the assigned children, including your own child.
- Read and follow the trip itinerary.
- Listen carefully for any special instructions from the head teacher.
- Upon return, wait with your group of children in a safe location until their family arrives for pickup.

Things to know:

Many children have allergies, therefore, bringing or purchasing food, treats or beverages for your assigned group is prohibited.

Chaperones may not bring siblings on the bus. If you have siblings and would like to attend the trip (not as a chaperone), the option of following the bus may be possible depending on the nature of the trip.

Families may drive their children home directly from the trip *if our release form is signed by the family member on the day of the trip.*

Smoking is prohibited on all trips.

How can I sign up?

- Look on your child's class information bulletin board for all upcoming trips.
- Sign-up sheets will be posted.
- If a spot is available, sign your name on the sign-up sheet.
- *Please notify us as soon as possible if you need to cancel.*

Chaperones are an important and valued part of the fun and success of our trips!
We thank you in advance for your help.

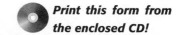

Print this form from the enclosed CD!

Chaperone Itinerary Template

Farmer's Market Itinerary
Thursday October 10, 2002

Chaperone: _____

Responsible for: _____   _____

_____   _____

_____   _____

IN CASE OF EMERGENCY CALL XXX-XXXX

7:00–9:30 Regular morning activities. Collect all lunches and place in the field trip bin. Each child will also be bringing a labeled water bottle on the trip. The chaperones will be responsible for carrying these water bottles. Also, if any child brings money to go to the country store, the chaperone will be responsible for placing the money in the provided envelope. *$5.00 is plenty for a child to bring on this trip.*

8:00–9:15 Snack in the art room

8:30–9:45 Clean up, take bathroom break, and gather children in the middle room. Make sure attendance is taken and have kids get into groups with their chaperone as soon as their name is called. Check for all lunches. Go over the following safety rules.

1. Stay with your group. Especially when completing the maze.
2. Listen to your chaperone at all times.
3. Be careful and aware of other groups completing the maze.

9:45–10:00 Final head count and board bus.

10:15 Depart center for Farmer's Market.

10:45–12:15 Arrive at Farmer's Market. We will be solving a story while completing the maze. The maze will take approximately 1 hour to complete. If you need more time, this can be allotted.

12:15–1:00 Lunch outside (weather permitting) on available picnic tables. Clean up after your group has finished and have children use the restrooms.

1:00–1:30 Children who have brought money on the trip can browse the country store. Chaperones should help children with their purchases.

1:30–1:45 If there is time remaining you can complete the smaller mazes that are located just outside the large maze.

1:45–2:00 All groups should gather at the picnic tables. This will allow for attendance before boarding the bus. *Bathrooms can be used now, before heading home.*

2:00 All children and chaperones will board the bus and depart for the center.

2:45 Approximate arrival time at center.

ACTIVITY 9.7 Creating a Field Trip Checklist

Using the template provided on page 163, create a customized checklist to be completed prior to each field trip. The checklist can be altered to accommodate the specific needs of each planned trip. The head teacher accompanying the group on the field trip should complete this checklist.

Access to emergency supplies may be limited depending on your destination. For this reason it is prudent to have the head teacher bring a basic first aid kit along for the trip. You should also bring the emergency contact cards of all of the participating children. Should a serious injury occur you will need to contact the family immediately and then access the physician contact information. These numbers should be listed on the family and emergency cards. If the bus is remaining at the field trip location you can leave these items on the bus. If the bus will not be staying you will need to designate a staff member to take responsibility for the emergency kit during the field trip. The person responsible for the first aid kit and emergency cards should also be the person who carries the cell phone.

With so much to remember on the day of a field trip, a checklist can be a useful tool to help organize your activities and ensure that everything is appropriately completed. While the specific needs of each field trip are different, you can create a checklist that addresses the common activities for all excursions away from the center.

Community Involvement

The final type of special event are those that are designed to promote *community involvement*. Community involvement involves a wide range of activities that allow interaction between different groups. The intention of the Helping Hands Program is to provide an opportunity for families to interact with their children's class. This program differs from the opportunity to chaperone a field trip as it allows families to see what a typical day for their child is like at the center. The program can be beneficial for all parties involved; families are able to get a firsthand look at how their child spends the day, staff members benefit from the relationship-building experience with the family member, and the children love having the chance to show off their family member to classmates.

The degree to which a family member chooses to participate in Helping Hands can vary. Some family members prefer to follow the teacher's activities and act as an aide for the day. Other family members might enjoy preparing a lesson of their own. Many family members have various talents and hobbies that would be of interest to the children. If they feel comfortable doing so, sharing these skills can be an exciting and valuable lesson.

Having a family member spend a day at the center in the classroom can be a valuable communication tool. The family member is able to get to know the teacher and her style of interaction with the children. Family members are often surprised at how much goes on during the day that demands the teacher's attention. The teacher also has an opportunity to learn more about the family member and his or her interests.

Field Trip Checklist Template

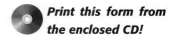

FIELD TRIP CHECKLIST

Check When Completed	
	Prior to the Trip
☐	Information sent to families 2–3 weeks in advance
☐	Chaperone sign-up posted 2–3 weeks in advance
☐	Information on trip placed in Coming Attractions newsletter one week before the trip
☐	Information on field trip posted on program bulletin board
☐	Itinerary prepared 1 week in advance and reviewed at staff meeting
☐	Children placed in groups with chaperones
☐	Chaperone name tags completed
☐	Safety rules reviewed with staff and children
	Day of the Trip
☐	Chaperones given name tags and itinerary
☐	Children introduced to chaperone
☐	Head teacher brings cell phone, first aid kit, and emergency cards
☐	Attendance and head count taken before boarding the bus No. Children _____ No. Staff _____ No. Chaperones _____ Total _____
☐	Children use bathroom prior to boarding the bus
☐	Chaperone has accounted for each child's lunch and other needed supplies
☐	Head count taken after bus has been boarded and children are secured Total _____
☐	Children use bathrooms prior to reboarding bus
☐	Head count taken prior to departure, number matches previous count Total _____
☐	First aid supplies, cell phone, emergency cards accounted for

ACTIVITY 9.8 Creating a Helping Hands Handout

To ensure that each child has an opportunity to spend the day with their family member at school, a handout on the program should be given to families at the start of the program. Using the template provided below, design a handout that provides your families with information on the Helping Hands Program.

Helping Hands Handout Template

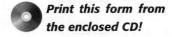 *Print this form from the enclosed CD!*

"Helping Hands" Family Interaction Program

Helping Hands is designed to give our families an opportunity to interact with their child's class. If you are interested in being involved in this program, please review the following information:

Why should I participate?

Children love to have their family members come to school to share in the experience. It makes them feel special and gives them a sense of pride to show you off to their friends and classmates.

How long do I stay?

This program is designed for the family member to stay the duration of their child's day. Staying from start to finish will give you the full experience of your child's routine.

What do I do?

We suggest family members become involved in the class activities for the day. Follow the teacher's planned activities if you like or take it a step further and bring in an activity or book to share with the class. We have had many parents share their talents with us in the form of cooking, planting, arts and crafts, music, reading, and various other hobbies.

How do I sign up?

Each teacher has a November–June calendar (with designated Helping Hands days highlighted) posted on the program bulletin board. Find the highlighted day in the month you would like to join us and sign your name in the book. It is that easy!

How many times can I sign up?

We ask that each family member who would like to participate sign up once during the school year. We would like to give each child the opportunity to have a family member come to the center. If all family members have had an opportunity to sign up and dates are still available, a second day can be scheduled.

We look forward to having you in the class!

Due to all of the new tasks that accompany the start of any new program, it may not be feasible to begin accepting Helping Hands volunteers until children have settled into the typical daily routines. Each staff member can determine when during the school year they would like to host classroom visitors. Prior to the day of the visit, the teacher and family member should discuss the plans for the day and make arrangements for any special materials the family member may need for his/her presentation.

Another aspect of community involvement special events is to introduce children to the idea of the world at large. It is easy for children to become focused on their own small communities. In order to help the children understand about all of the groups within the wider community they may not have had the opportunity to meet, you can arrange community service projects. Instead of donating money the children can donate their time and good wishes. A great idea for a community service special event is Valentines for Veterans.

In addition to creating Valentine greetings for their family and classmates, the children can make special cards for people who also deserve remembering during this holiday. Most communities have a Veteran's Association who are happy to provide the names of veterans who may not have many family members or visitors. You can also consider making Valentine's cards for the residents of a local nursing home. During the card making, you should discuss the importance of the elderly with the children. Ask the children to share any memories they have about their grandparents or other older family friends. You can encourage the children to ask their families about anyone they might know who has served our country. Learning about different generations can help to foster a respect for all others in our communities.

Families like to know that their children have the opportunity to engage in a wide variety of special events while in your care. Special events provide numerous opportunities for interaction and communication among your audiences. Families, staff, children, and the community are able to learn more about each other all while having fun.

Communication Progress Report

Skill or Task	Range of Abilities		
	ALWAYS MEET	EMERGING SKILL	WILL IMPROVE
An Open House has been planned to provide a warm introduction to the center and staff.	☐	☐	☐
Family Orientation Night covers all of the necessary information relating to the center and program.	☐	☐	☐
Families leave Family Orientation Night feeling as though they made the right choice in enrolling their child in the center.	☐	☐	☐
Staff members proactively establish communication with families at the informational special events.	☐	☐	☐
The children in each program have the opportunity to participate in several performances throughout the year.	☐	☐	☐
Information regarding performances has been given to families in plenty of time for them to prepare for the event.	☐	☐	☐
Children enjoy taking an active role in the planned performances.	☐	☐	☐
The curriculum is enhanced by a variety of special events occurring within and outside the center.	☐	☐	☐
Checklists and itineraries are designed for each curriculum-enhancing special event.	☐	☐	☐
Roles and responsibilities for those participating in special events have been clearly defined and communicated.	☐	☐	☐
Events have been designed to bring communities into the classroom.	☐	☐	☐
Each special event planned is a good experience for all involved.	☐	☐	☐

10

Getting the Word Out: Effective Advertisement and Marketing

COMMUNICATION

COMING ATTRACTIONS

- How to distinguish the various components that will make up your marketing strategy

- How to create advertisements that will leave your audience wanting to learn more

- How to harness the power of community activities to promote your center

How do you effectively communicate to an audience that you may not have any direct contact with? You know potential families and students are out there, but how do you find them? How can you make them notice you? Will they remember you? Those are the big questions for any industry. There are many multimillion-dollar companies that have large budgets strictly devoted to advertising and marketing their products or services. A fraction of this budget will cost more than most child care businesses will ever see in profits. This chapter will discuss ways that you can target your audiences in a manner that will suit your business.

Knowing the difference between marketing and advertising is sometimes confusing. They both play a key role in the growth of your business and although the terms are often used interchangeably their definitions are not identical. It is important to understand the whole concept in order to make this process work effectively for you. A business description between the differences of the two terms would be as follows:

Marketing: An organized plan to bring together a group or individuals of potential buyers to existing sellers for a mutual transfer of goods and services.

Advertisement: A paid public announcement to attract potential and existing customers to its product.

Marketing Strategy

Using an example that we all would understand, try to envision a rainbow. Think of how the many different rays of colors make up the arc. Although each color is separate the combined effect is what makes the image breathtaking. The dramatic image of a rainbow will be remembered and talked about for some time to come. In this analogy the rainbow is marketing and the individual rays are all of the different components of marketing. Our rainbow has five different colors, all corresponding the five components that make up a marketing strategy. These components are:

Advertisement

Public Relations: The daily positive interactions between administrators, staff, and families. Public relations include ongoing activities to ensure the company has a strong image within the community. Public relations activities are designed to help the public to understand the company and its services.

Promotion: Promotion keeps the product in the minds of the customer and helps stimulate demand for the services. Handing out hats or t-shirts with the center logo would be promotional activities.

Market Analysis and Research: Reaching the community in order to assess need for your services. These activities will help to determine your business environment and may provide you with information about the type of marketing campaign that will be most effective for your business.

Sales: The activities that lead up to enrollment of new children.

Marketing takes on the bigger picture of acquainting the public to your business. This is a long-term endeavor that will require a great deal of time and patience. It also depends upon the level of commitment to help decide the amount of time needed to put your marketing plan into place. There are many different ways to establish your center in the marketplace. The most effective ways for the child care industry will be the ones that are most directly related to children and their families. The quality of the school's marketing plan can have a significant effect on the image it wants to project. The way you use this plan will hopefully have a lasting impact on all of your audiences.

When you initially sit down and try to decide, "How will I let the community know about my school?" You immediately think, "I'll run an advertisement in the paper!" Advertisement is the most widely used method in the child care industry and it is usually the most expensive. However, it is important to remember that while advertisement is important, it is only one part of the total marketing process. Advertisement is only one color of our rainbow, and therefore should not be the sole focus of your time and money.

Print Advertising

The written word is the most commonly used form of advertisement for the child care industry. This can be used as a powerful tool for the success of your business. The presentation of these words can be achieved in many different ways. This is usually accomplished by advertisements placed in newspapers, on bulletin boards, magazines, flyers, bulk mailings, telephone books, and calendars. Equally important forms of advertisements and marketing to consider are radio and television representation, the Internet, and word of mouth. You will need to consider all of these forms of media before you decide how to advertise and market your business. The advertisement method your choose should reach the widest number of potential families.

Before you can determine which method of advertisement will have the maximum impact, you need to consider your target audience. Geographical location is important. Are the families you want to reach all within a few miles radius of your school? If so, advertising in a large metropolitan newspaper may not be your best resource. In this situation you are likely to receive more exposure by placing your advertisement in a local paper. Many communities have small local newspapers that are less costly than larger metropolitan papers. In addition, you are more likely to receive guidance in developing a print advertisement when working with the staff of a smaller paper.

Try to come up with an idea that is unique and appeals to your target audiences. You want the images that you choose to invoke positive feelings in the people viewing them. Those reading the ads will then associate the positive feelings with your center. The very nature of the child care business makes this step an easy one. People universally experience positive emotions when viewing pictures of happy children. Your business has an ample supply of beautiful and endearing children. What better way to get people to look for your ads than with the use of pictures of children from your school. People are especially drawn to images that have captured emotion. The image that seems to work best is a simple candid close-up of an individual child. The

**Example of a General Advertisement Using
Pictures of Children from Your Center**

expressions that children make are priceless, and sometimes we are lucky enough to capture one on film.

You will have the families looking at the advertisement, the children, the neighbors, virtually everyone who picks up the paper. This is one method that never seems to grow old. Currently enrolled families will look each time to see which child is featured. Children love collecting the pictures of themselves and their friends. Family members will ask neighbors to save their newspaper clippings for them. Before you know it, you have the whole community involved in your advertisement. For many months to come you will see these ads taped to the refrigerator doors to be seen and shared with family and friends. Not only is it a great source of exposure for your school, it is also a way to communicate with your current families the happy faces you see throughout the center.

The majority of families can't wait for the opportunity to see a picture of their child in the newspaper. However, requesting permission in writing for the use of a child's picture is an important step that must not be overlooked. There are many legitimate reasons as to why a parent does not want their child's picture published. Give the families an opportunity to see the picture in print before sending it off to the newspaper. Never assume that because you like a picture that the family will like it as well.

ACTIVITY 10.1 Creating a Permission Form for Photograph Use

Use the template provided below to customize a permission form for use of a photograph. Always attach a copy of the intended photograph to this form.

Print this form from the enclosed CD!

Permission for Photograph Use Template

Date:

Dear Family _____

I love this photograph of your child. Some time in the near future I would like to use this picture of [insert child's name] in an advertisement for the center. Please give me your signature as your sign of approval.

Sincerely,

I agree to allow   [Name of School]   to use this picture of

[Child's Name]   as a form of commercial advertisement for the school.

Signature: _____

Date: _____

See reverse side for copy of photo

If you decide that exposure beyond your immediate community is necessary in order to attract a wider range of families, a larger metropolitan newspaper may be the answer for you. Evaluate the timing of the publication and method to be used. Call the newspaper about publication packages. Most newspapers offer discount rates for the number of times you advertise. They also offer special packages for different times of the year. There is almost always a special flyer that is designated for summer camp programs and a fall "going back to school" issue. Utilize these special additions to your advantage. Come up with something that the public will remember. When you advertise in a metropolitan paper you need to expect that a significant number of other centers will also be advertising in the issue. You need to design an advertisement that catches the viewer's eye.

171

Example of an Advertisement Letting Your Community Know about Specific Programs

Marketing in the Community

You will need to be creative in your marketing strategy. Print advertisements alone may not be sufficient to attract the number of families you need to grow your business. Your community offers a wealth of possibilities for promotional and public relation activities. Some of the more tried and true methods of expanding the marketing of your business are involvements with:

- Welcome Wagon
- trade shows
- corporate events
- real estate agencies
- Helping Hands agencies
- charities
- library programs

WHEN COMMUNICATION BREAKS DOWN

Ad Copy:

A LOVING LOCAL FAMILY
HOME DAY CARE CENTER
HAS ROOM FOR

1
INFANT

OUTCOME: The small child care facility spent their entire monthly advertising budget by placing an ad in a large metropolitan paper. The spot available for infant care remained open.

LESSON LEARNED: A more practical approach would be to advertise in a local newspaper once a week for a month. The local paper may have also had a reduced rate allowing for a picture to be included along with the text. This ad would be very easily overlooked in any newspaper.

- church programs and functions
- play groups
- scholarship funds
- newcomers clubs

Involvement within the community is an excellent way to establish and promote your school. In most cases your business is located within the community in which you live. Your children may attend the school, participate in league games, and sell raffle tickets for various fund-raisers. Family members may work in the area, attend the churches, or support local business. This makes it a perfect bridge for your involvement. The local Parent Teacher Organization (PTO) is always looking for items for their annual fund-raisers. A raffle item representing your school could consist of a t-shirt, hat, or water bottle with your logo, and a certificate for a free program registration. The fund-raising committee would appreciate this item, and it would be a great marketing tool.

Another example of how to make inroads into your community through marketing and advertisement is the center's support of the other local agencies, organizations, and businesses. Plan an event that would require you to ask for community assistance. For example, if a new bicycle shop recently opened up in your community you can offer to support their new business by placing flyers in your center's lobby. In return they could donate a new bike to be raffled off at the center's special event. The bike could be prominently displayed at the school with accompanying advertisements for the bike shop. This will create a lot of talk and excitement among the children and families.

EFFECTIVE COMMUNICATION IN ACTION

A community has organized a very active newcomers group. The organization has been involved in various fund-raising and charitable activities for the local area. This year they decided to establish a "Dress for Success" fund for all children entering the first grade. To ensure that all children were equipped with the proper learning materials, they solicited area businesses for pledges of money and support. The local child care center not only pledged to outfit two children, it established a wishing well fund for new pencils and other needed school supplies. The children could donate money for the purchases by throwing coins into a well.

OUTCOME: The children entering the first grade all received the needed supplies for the beginning of school. The school received local notoriety for their involvement. The children enjoyed helping others and also enjoyed throwing money into the well. They are excited to hold the fund-raiser again next year.

Pictures should be taken of the actual raffle drawing and of the winning child. These pictures can be given to the local newspaper as an advertisement for both the bike shop and the center. Because it was a community event, the advertisement is usually free for both the school and the bike shop.

Families and children are usually eager to participate in activities where they feel they are making a contribution to their community. Establish some type of yearly fund-raiser where all of the profits go directly to the designated organization. One way to accomplish this is to include in your weekly planning an event called "Pizza Friday." The proceeds of this event should be adequate to maintain your Community Outreach Fund. The children will be able to enjoy pizza every Friday at a low cost to their families. If you are able to establish a sharing and working relationship with the owner of the local pizza shop, the pizzas can be purchased at a reduced price. The accumulated money at the end of the month can be donated on behalf of the families of your center.

Making a long-term commitment to an organization such as a senior citizen facility will have a lasting impact for all of those involved. With the weekly donations from your Pizza Fridays, the seniors can use the donated money to purchase needed supplies or hold social events. This relationship can be furthered by planning field trips for the children to visit the residents of the senior center. The children can work with the residents with the supplies purchased through the donated monies. The event can be captured on film and the pictures and story sent to the local newspaper.

Any of your staff members who have an interest in public speaking should be encouraged to volunteer their services at events. Groups such as "Mommy and Me" are always open to have professional educators present informal seminars on issues of child development. Although you may not be speaking about your center directly, participation in these events will get the center name out into the community. When an

Example of an Advertisement That Lets Your Audience Know of Your Community Involvements

"Kids on the Go" at Bright Beginnings

Bright Beginnings "Kids on the Go" joins residents of the community to make holiday windsocks as part of the Artists program. Bright Beginnings has been coordinating these activities for the past three years.

Bright Beginnings students are working with their friends and the community to make this a great event. "Personally, I truly enjoyed the fact that the children introduced the residents as their friends!" commented the head teacher.

It's smiles all around for Bright Beginnings "Kids on the Go" and the residents of the community. They got together to do a holiday craft on October 2.

individual in the audience needs child care services, they will likely remember the name of your center.

Most local park and recreation programs offer babysitting classes for teenagers. As someone with education and experience in the field of child care, you are an ideal teacher for a course of this nature. These teenagers would benefit from discussion about real-life scenarios that occur when caring for children. Development of a hands-on training program for future babysitters is a worthwhile experience for all involved. Not only are you helping to safeguard the children of your community, you are also helping to associate the name of your center with caring and community involvement. It is also likely that some of the teens that attend your program will have younger family members who could use your services.

A highly visible and convenient method of community involvement is the establishment of a newspaper column. Local experts in their field could write this column. Doctors, dentists, psychologists, educators, nutritionists, and members of the school board all have important contributions to make in the field of child care. As long as the content is relevant to children, you can be creative in the choice of authors. The topics could vary based on current events and the needs of the community. For example, the

Example of a Newspaper Column

Today's Kids
by
Mary Arnold

Is It Really Stealing?

Almost every parent has had to deal with a child who has taken something that didn't belong to him or her. Usually these episodes occur when the children are preschoolers and haven't quite mastered the concepts of "ownership" and "stealing." Often, very young preschoolers can't distinguish between fact and fantasy, either. They may take something in the context of a pretend game, never realizing they are taking something from a friend. Parental reaction to this childhood stealing is fairly universal—the child is made to return the item in question (or pay for the item) and is lectured on why stealing is wrong.

Then the kids get a little older. What happens when your middle-school age child swipes candy from a convenience store? You'd probably react the same way you did when they were a preschooler—have him or her return the merchandise or pay for it, and apologize to the store's owner.

We're telling our kids that stealing is wrong, but what are we saying with our actions? Doing the right thing is as important as saying the right thing when it comes to your children and ethics. If you're given back too much change at the grocery store do you give it back or do you keep it? Do most of your home office supplies actually come from your office?

In one scenario, as told by a sixth grader, his family moved into a new house. The cable television outlets were "hot" and the family received cable television without paying. Actually they received cable TV for eight years before the company caught up with them. The child's response was, "the cable company was stupid for not turning off the cable." The child sees absolutely nothing wrong with using cable for eight years without paying. From listening to the story, you can guess the parents' "view" from listening to this subject. In my book this is simply stealing.

Another family, when planning a party felt that their home needed some additional decorating. The couple went out and purchased coffee and end tables, and several accessories. Once the party was over, the furniture and accessories were returned to the store because they didn't "work in the room." Is this stealing?

The merchandise was returned, hopefully in the same condition that it was "purchased," so what's the harm? Since the couple had no intention of keeping the items, only "borrowing" them for the party, I consider this stealing, too. With the merchandise out of the store, the merchant might have lost the sale of a legitimate buyer. As we've discussed in previous columns, children are great imitators. Our children's moral compass is formed as much by our actions as by our words. It's very difficult to maintain credibility with your children when you are saying one thing (stealing is wrong) and then doing the opposite.

National Public Radio broadcast a recent feature about theft in restaurants. One young woman interviewed for the story admitted to taking over 70 pairs of salt and pepper shakers from all over the world. She didn't consider it stealing and said that if she were caught she'd say, "OOPS, it fell into my purse."

Another person interviewed for this story said that she learned the art of stealing from restaurants from her mother who routinely took items from restaurants. Restaurant owners say they've lost everything from silverware, dishes, and salt shakers to chairs, antique lavatory faucets and other pieces of furniture and artwork.

Buying your office supplies at a store, rather than bringing them home from your office and paying for the goods and services you use, illustrates to your children how to live and get along in society. Doing the right thing is the right thing to do and it's the right thing to do to raise honest, ethical children.

The article was written by Mary Arnold, Executive Director of Bright Beginnings.

local dentist could be asked to submit an article during Dental Health Month. For Halloween, you could ask the local police departments to lend their name and offer published materials concerning candy safety and on how to safeguard children walking alone at night. A newspaper column will require a great time commitment and you should be prepared for this before you undertake such an endeavor. Families will come to look for your articles in the paper and will ask questions if you stop the publications. In the interest of public relations, it is best to stay away from topics that can cause controversy. You want your newspaper column to be used as a vehicle for information and communication, not expression of opinions.

The Welcome Wagon is a very direct method of reaching your targeted audience. You can request that the Welcome Wagon representative only provide information concerning your school to new families that move into the area with children. The representative would leave a useful token of remembrance about your school with each house call. A pencil or pen left behind should have the inscription of your center on it. The agency currently provides each new family with a telephone directory with local businesses listed in the directory. For an additional charge your center can be listed in the directory under the listing of "Schools or Child Care Centers." As a method of follow-up, take the monthly lists of contacts provided by the Welcome Wagon and send each family additional information concerning your center and the programs you offer.

Real estate agencies welcome ways to interest new buyers into the community. A brochure included in a potential buyer packet about a local child care center could possibly entice the house buyer to request more information. In designing this brochure, keep in mind possible multiple uses of this material. If you list the type of programs you offer without any specific use in mind it can also be used in your training manuals, handouts, and bulk mailing.

Advertising On-Line

The Internet is a novel and exciting way to access information about the child care industry. The U.S. population is becoming more aware of the advantages of using the Internet for research. Child care centers are starting to develop their own Web sites that can be accessed by current or potential families. For the families that are currently enrolled in your center the Web site would provide information. New families moving into the area can obtain information about the school before leaving their current area. The development of your own Web site can be a costly undertaking, and you will need technical skills to develop one on your own. Before beginning the process of building a Web page, think about your target audience. Do many of them have access to a computer and the Internet? If not, building a Web site may not be the best investment for your advertising dollar.

Just as you would when you put together print media you need to think about the content of your Web page. What are you trying to accomplish? Remember that the information contained in your Web page will be accessible to readers around the world. Before you can begin building you will need to put together a plan for your Web site. Normally, in Web site designing, people term a Web site plan as a sitemap (Web site map). You can even add this plan to your Web site after it is completed so people are able to see on one page everything that is contained within the site. If you are not sure what type of information to include you can take a look at the sitemaps and Web sites of other schools. It is a general rule that people do not read lengthy documents posted on the Web. You will need to rework the type of information you would like to include on your Web site so it is informational but succinct. The layout should be simple and easily read; you will want to include graphics that make your page interesting.

Once you have developed the content of the Web page, you will need to convert the files into a form that can be read over the Internet. Text files will need to be converted into HyperText Markup Language (HTML), and your graphics will need to be in JPEG or GIF format. Although this may sound like a daunting task, it doesn't have to be. Many Microsoft Word programs can do the conversion for you. There are many books and programs that you can buy that will provide you with more information on the nuts

BRIGHT BEGINNINGS...
THE RIGHT DECISION FOR CHILD CARE

Bright Beginnings, New Fairfield's premier child care facility, offers innovative programs to meet the needs of your busy family. With all our programs, your child will grow and learn important new skills every day in a safe, loving environment. They won't think of it as learning... just as fun!

HALF-DAY PRESCHOOL
- Three- and four-year-old classes with morning and afternoon sessions
- Developmentally appropriate curriculum
- Enrichment course for academically advanced fours

FULL-DAY PRESCHOOL
- Same outstanding curriculum as the half-day students
- Additional enrichment activities and special programs
- Hours that fit your schedule 7:00 a.m. to 6:00 p.m.
- A warm, loving home-away-from-home

FULL-DAY KINDERGARTEN
- Small class size   • Individual attention for all students
- Curriculum includes math, language arts, reading, social studies, science, art & music
- Includes before and after school care

"KIDS ON THE GO"
- Before and after school program
- Stimulating activities in art, music, fitness
- Theme weeks-cooking, crafts & more
- Exciting, age-appropriate field trips

SUMMER CAMP
A wide variety of optional programs
- Gymnastics • Computers
- Tae Kwon Do • Dance

Taught by professionals who bring their programs to the center (additional fees associated with these activities)

BRIGHT BEGINNINGS FACILITIES
- Bright, open preschool classrooms
- Professional teaching staff
- Age-appropriate, stimulating equipment
- New self-contained Kindergarten classroom
- Computer Lab-Library/Media Center-Science Lab

- Security system
- Small classes
- Private outdoor playground
- Field trips and special in-house programs

Example of a Child Care Brochure

BRIGHT
BEGINNINGS
the right decision

and bolts of putting together your first Web site. Be sure that you request a program for beginners. A comprehensive resource for beginners is *Building a School Website: A Hands-on Project for Teachers and Kids* (Independent Publisher's Group, 2000) by Wanda Wigglebits. You can purchase the book at a bookstore and may also access the information at http://www.wigglebits.com.

Once you have developed your Web page, you will need to find a place for it to reside. Your Web page must be placed on a Web server that is hooked up to the Internet 24 hours a day. You will need to do some research on this area. Look for a reliable and customer-friendly Web-hosting service. Prices can vary drastically from one host to another, so be sure to request complete information about the up-front and monthly costs. Ask potential hosting companies for the Web site address of other pages they host and spend some time surfing these sites. You will be looking for an easy, fast, and reliable connection to their other sites. Ask the hosting company if they are able to provide you with the domain name that you desire. Your first choice for a Web site address may be taken, so come up with several alternatives. The best addresses are those that are succinct and easy to remember. Some hosting services will only be able to provide you with long and cumbersome addresses; these do not look professional and should be avoided. Finally ask about the security the Web host provides. The host should be continually monitoring for suspicious behavior and should have in place systems to deter hackers.

Don't think that your job is finished once you have your Web site on-line and running. You are now responsible for maintenance of the site and the information it contains. You will need to check your site regularly to ensure that the files you have posted are working correctly and any links that you have made are still functioning. Also be sure that you update the Web site anytime information has been changed. A Web site that contains different information than your print media does looks careless and is likely to cause confusion and headaches.

If all of this sounds like too technical an investment for you, there are several companies that have packages designed to plan, develop, program, and maintain your Web site. Be sure to get several offers before making a decision, all costs should be in writing. Each phase of the development should come with an hourly rate and a cap indicating the maximum amount you are willing to spend.

There are alternative methods to provide Internet representation for your center. You can do this through the Better Business Bureau, the telephone yellow pages, and the national early childhood accreditation programs for NAEYC and NACCP. All of these agencies will list your business in their directory of membership, and many will give a detailed description of the services you provide. Some of these listings will be done at no cost to you.

A good resource for more information about the information superhighway is http://www.learnthenet.com. The "How To" section of this Web page provides support for everything from building a Web page to accessing e-mail.

Communication Progress Report

Skill or Task	Range of Abilities		
	ALMOST ALWAYS	**EMERGING SKILL**	**WILL LEARN**
I can identity the five components of marketing.	☐	☐	☐
Market research has been performed to determine the most effective means of reaching potential families.	☐	☐	☐
Print advertisements are both visually appealing and informative.	☐	☐	☐
Families must give written permission prior to their child's picture being used for advertisement purposes.	☐	☐	☐
The center is represented at a number of community events and involvements.	☐	☐	☐
Staff members are encouraged to participate in events that could generate positive press for the center.	☐	☐	☐
The center has strong collaborative relationships with other businesses that are seeking to attract families.	☐	☐	☐
New families to the area have a means of receiving information about the center.	☐	☐	☐
Families who have not currently moved to your area can research the center through the Internet.	☐	☐	☐
All affiliates of the center are aware that everything they do or say can be seen as potential advertisement for the center, either positive or negative.	☐	☐	☐

Summary

The concepts and activities presented throughout this text were designed to guide you in developing your own style of effective communication. It is important to remember that with each interaction, whether formal or informal, you are actively communicating with your audience.

Learning how to be an effective communicator takes both time and practice. While it can be a difficult skill to master, once you achieve it, you will find yourself both a better professional and a better educator. You need to go beyond "saying what you mean and meaning what you say." A child care professional must analyze different situations and choose from a variety of communication strategies. Although verbal communication may be the most common form, it is by no means the only one. If you are having a difficult time getting your message across using one method, try another. You will need to learn to adapt your skills to best meet the needs of your audience.

A final word of advice is to practice your communication skills daily. Let your peers know that you are working to become a more effective communicator. Elicit feedback, both positive and negative, from them. When told that your message was not well understood, ask how you could have done better. Let your confidence in yourself and your message shine through. Remember, each time you walk into a room, the most important component of your message is yourself!

Index